RECIPES FOR THE HEART

RECIPES FOR THE HEART
A Nutrition & Health Guide for People with High Blood Pressure

Lucy M. Williams, R.D.

Cover Design and Illustrations by
Tom C. Williams

Sandridge Publishing
Bowling Green, Ohio

Additional copies of this book may be ordered through bookstores or
by sending $13.50 plus $2.00 for postage and handling to:
Publishers Distribution Service
121 East Front Street, Suite 203
Traverse City, MI 49684
1-800-345-0096

Third printing 1992

Publisher's Cataloging-in-Publication Data

Williams, Lucy M., 1942-
  Recipes for the heart: a nutrition & health guide for people with high blood
pressure / Lucy M. Williams – 3rd Edition – Bowling Green, Ohio: Sandridge
Pub., 1990.

  x, 216 p.: ill.; cm.

  Includes bibliographical references and indexes.

  ISBN: 0-945080-42-5

  1. Hypertension – Diet therapy – Recipes. 2. Salt-free diet – Recipes. 3. Low-
cholesterol diet – Recipes. 4. Hypertension – Popular works. I. Title.

RC684.D5W55   641.5′63′11 – dc20   91-67851

Manufactured in the United States of America

ACKNOWLEDGMENTS

Without the support and talents of many people this book would not have been possible. I would like to thank Tom Williams who helped transform a dream into a reality through his artistic talents; my family who tested many recipes; Agnes and Edward Najam for sharing recipes and editing talents; Susan Barber who spent countless hours reshaping, editing, and smoothing rough words into meaningful text; Pat Peterson for material contributed to the exercise chapter; Harriet Randall for her typing skills, patience, and extra effort through all three editions; Sooja Kim who was instrumental in developing my interest in hypertension; and especially Lucille Merritt, a mother who has offered a lifetime of support and encouragement.

TABLE OF CONTENTS

INTRODUCTION

When your doctor diagnoses you as having high blood pressure (hypertension), you probably still feel fine physically. Mentally, however, you may be confused. Why should I take medicine or change my diet when I don't feel sick? What causes high blood pressure? How serious is it? These are just some of the questions you may have. Clearly, the more you understand about high blood pressure and its treatment, the easier it will be for you to control it.

Recipes For The Heart was written to help you understand high blood pressure and the dietary changes that may mean better control for you. The importance of each nutrient in the control of hypertension is explained; charts and selected recipes are included to help you choose foods responsibly as you work toward lowering your blood pressure.

Additional chapters help you make wise choices at restaurants and fast food chains, help in weight control and exercise, and make recommendations for efficient use of the microwave oven.

A word about the recipes:

HOMEMADE VS. PACKAGED. Most of the recipes in this book are very basic and can be prepared quickly. Too often basic recipes are forgotten and replaced with convenience foods. For example, cornbread is seldom made from scratch today; most often a box mix is used. You will discover as you try these recipes how much control you can have over the sodium content of your food when you learn to "make it from scratch." (You will also discover how much money you save by using your own ingredients instead of packaged ones.)

SPICES. Be flexible about the recommended spices; substitute your favorites as long as they don't contain salt. Reduce or omit entirely the spices you don't like. Regular commercial catsup and mustard have been used in recipes. To further reduce the sodium content of recipes, substitute the homemade catsup or mustard on page 26 and 25 respectively.

VEGETABLES AND FRUITS. Use fresh or frozen vegetables and fruits whenever possible. If canned items are used, the vegetables should be low-sodium and the fruits should be canned in their own juices.

LOW-FAT DAIRY PRODUCTS. Always use low-fat dairy products such as skim or 1 percent milk; if 1 percent is not available, mix equal parts of 2 percent and skim milk. High-fat dairy products should not be substituted for these ingredients; doing so will alter the nutrient content of the recipe. Use vegetable oil sprays to coat muffin, cookie, and cake pans instead of greasing with oil or butter.

SALT. Salt is included as an ingredient in many recipes. The purpose of this book is to make you aware of all the possible sources of salt and how to control it in your diet, not necessarily to convince you to omit it altogether. For example, if you are trying to restrict your daily intake of sodium to 2,000 mg (one teaspoon of salt) and you have consumed very small amounts in a particular day, you may want to add an extra pinch to the vegetable-cheese soup you made for dinner. Learn to use salt wisely.

LEFTOVERS? If recipes are too large, cut the ingredients in half for a smaller portion or freeze the leftovers for another meal.

HYPERTENSION

WHAT IS HYPERTENSION?

Hypertension, the medical term for high blood pressure, is often called "the silent disease" because you can have high blood pressure for years without knowing it. Many people are surprised to learn that they can have hypertension without feeling sick. Hypertension is not a disease; rather, it is a symptom. Therefore it cannot be cured, but **it can be controlled.** Medication, dietary changes, weight loss, stress reduction, and exercise may all work toward lowering blood pressure. In addition, tobacco products should be avoided and alcohol consumption should be limited.

When your blood pressure returns to normal you are not at the end of your struggle but rather, the beginning! Whatever method or combination of methods you used, you must continue for the rest of your life.

BLOOD PRESSURE DEFINED

There must be pressure to move the blood from the heart through the vessels to the body's organs and cells. The blood vessels can become larger (*dilate*) or smaller (*constrict*), depending on the demands put upon them. Normally, blood flows easily through the vessels. But, if the blood vessels narrow too much, the heart must pump harder to push blood through. This extra effort increases the pressure on the inside of the walls. Many of the complications of hypertension are a result of this increased pressure.

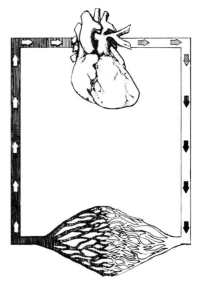

MEASUREMENT OF BLOOD PRESSURE

Blood pressure is measured with a *sphygmomanometer*. A cuff is wrapped around the upper arm over the artery. The cuff is then inflated with air by squeezing the bulb. Pressure in the cuff causes the artery walls to compress against each other so there is no blood flow. When this occurs, no pulse can be heard  with a stethoscope. As the pressure in the cuff is slowly released, a stethoscope is used to detect the sound of a pulse as blood starts to flow through the artery. At the first sound of a pulse, the sphygmomanometer dial is read indicating the *systolic* pressure. The systolic pressure is a measurement of the heart as it pumps under pressure. When a pulse is no longer heard, a second number, indicating the *diastolic* pressure, is recorded. The diastolic pressure is a measurement of the heart at rest. Blood pressure is written in numbers such as 120/80. The top number indicates systolic pressure; the bottom indicates diastolic pressure.

Normal blood pressure readings -	
less than 140 systolic	less than 85 diastolic
Borderline high blood pressure readings -	
140 to 159 systolic	85 to 89 diastolic
High blood pressure readings -	
160 or over systolic	90 or over diastolic*
*90 - 104 diastolic is considered mild 105 - 114 diastolic is considered moderate 115 and over diastolic is considered severe	

WHAT CAUSES HYPERTENSION?

In most cases of hypertension (90 to 95 percent), a specific cause cannot be found. However, hypertension may be linked to:

- **heredity.** If one parent has hypertension, a child has an increased risk. If two parents have high blood pressure the risks are even greater.

- **blood vessels** that narrow or enlarge more than they should.

- **kidneys** that can't rid the body of excess sodium. Sodium attracts extra water in the blood stream, making the heart work harder to push the increased volume through the blood vessels.

- **other factors** such as obesity, smoking, race, age, alcohol consumption, and oral contraceptive use.

- **high-sodium diets.** About one-third of those who have high blood pressure are sensitive to dietary sodium. Because it is difficult to determine who is sensitive to sodium, most individuals with high blood pressure are placed on low-salt diets.

- **low dietary potassium and calcium intakes.** As with sodium, only a certain percentage of individuals may be affected. Thus, adequate amounts of potassium and calcium are important in the diets of all hypertensive people.

COMPLICATIONS OF HIGH BLOOD PRESSURE

It is extremely important to control high blood pressure because of complications called "risk factors" that may develop. The most serious risk factors involve the:

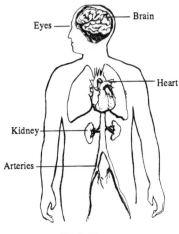

Risk Factors

- **heart.** The heart has to work harder to push blood through narrowed vessels or to push increased amounts of fluids through normal blood vessels. Like any muscle, the heart enlarges when it is overworked. After years of overwork, the heart can no longer work efficiently and eventually fails. **Hypertension is the major cause of heart failure.**

- **brain.** When vessels that carry blood to the brain are narrowed, the brain cells can't get enough oxygen to function. In addition, brain vessels aren't protected with tissue like other body vessels, and therefore, burst easier under increased pressure. **Hypertension is a primary cause of strokes.**

- **kidneys.** If vessels are hardened, body wastes can't be removed effectively and build up in the blood. **Kidney damage can occur from hypertension.**

- **eyes.** Blood vessels in the eye are constantly strained and swollen from high blood pressure. This leads to swelling and tiny breaks in the blood vessels of the retina. **Hypertension can lead to blindness.**

- **arteries.** Nature's attempt to withstand increased pressure in the arteries is to thicken the interior walls of the vessels. The vessels thus narrow as the walls become thicker. The increased pressure pushes fatty deposits into artery walls. The arteries become less elastic and lack "stretchiness" due to the deposits. **Atherosclerosis, or hardening of the arteries, results from hypertension.**

TREATMENT OF HYPERTENSION

There are several different methods that may be used in the effort to lower high blood pressure. Your physician may recommend specific dietary changes as well as regular exercise and possibly a weight loss program and a stress management program. Under no circumstances should a person with high blood pressure use tobacco products. Drinking of alcohol should be limited to one or two ounces a day.

Dietary Changes. For many hypertensive individuals it is not necessary to treat the high blood pressure with drugs. Diet alone will reduce blood pressure satisfactorily. For those who do not respond to dietary changes alone, a combination of prescribed medication along with a carefully controlled diet will have to be implemented. It is important to realize that some high blood pressure medications have side effects that might include increased blood levels of glucose, cholesterol, and triglycerides. For that reason, people on high blood pressure medication should limit simple sugars and fatty foods. In addition, diuretics, which are prescribed by hypertensive people in order to decrease excess fluids, result in losses of potassium and calcium. A good balance of all nutrients must be maintained with an appropriate diet.

7

Regular Exercise. Exercise helps to control blood pressure by reducing the fat in the blood stream, decreasing stress, burning calories, and conditioning the heart. Exercise also makes weight loss easier.

Weight Reduction. Extra weight means extra work for the heart. It takes two miles of capillaries to nourish one pound of fat. Weight reduction, if needed, can often reduce blood pressure a great deal.

Stress Reduction. Stress is a part of everyday living for all people. Too much stress can affect mental and physical well-being resulting in headaches, insomnia, high blood pressure, and many other ailments.

Smoking Cessation. Nicotine is a drug that raises blood pressure by making the heart beat faster at the same time that it constricts the blood vessels. Don't smoke!

Alcohol Control. Alcohol is a drug that may raise blood pressure in some individuals. Limit your alcohol consumption to one or two ounces a day.

Antihypertensive Medications. The most common drug used in the initial treatment of hypertension is a *diuretic*. Diuretics reduce the fluid content of the blood and body by increasing the urine output. The increased urine output results in sodium losses because sodium is attracted to water. Potassium is also lost, however, and is replaced through supplements or by increasing dietary sources of potassium. Physicians may prescribe a *potassium-sparing diuretic* that prevents potassium losses but may not be as effective in lowering blood pressure.

Many other antihypertensive drugs are used by physicians to control hypertension. Some of the drugs are used to slow down the heart beat, to open (dilate) blood vessels, or to act on the nervous system directly.

Most physicians use the *step-treatment* form of therapy when administering antihypertensive drugs. Step-treatment is therapy that starts with a small dosage of an antihypertensive drug, in most cases a diuretic. If blood pressure control does not result, the dosage may be increased or another antihypertensive drug may be added. Should side effects develop, one drug can be substituted for another. In the same way, if the maximum dose of one drug is reached and blood pressure control hasn't been achieved, another can be added.

Many antihypertensive drugs have side effects. *Always notify your physician about possible side effects and never try to change dosages on your own.*

Over-the Counter Drugs. Many over-the-counter products contain labels warning individuals with high blood pressure to avoid their use. This is because they may cause the blood vessels to constrict (get smaller). The heart may have to work harder to push blood through smaller vessels causing blood pressure to increase. Cough medicines and decongestants are the most common drugs to carry these warnings. A partial list of these medications follows, but always read labels on any over-the-counter drugs. Contact your physician or pharmacist if questions occur.

Allerest (tablets)
Benadryl (decongestant & cold formula tablets)
Chlor-Trimeton (tablet & expectorant)
CONTAC (cold)
Novahistine (most products, check labels)
Robitussin (check labels)
Sinutab (tablet)
Sudafed
Thera Flu
Triaminic (check labels)
Tylenol Cold
Vicks Sinex

ANTIHYPERTENSIVE DRUGS

Drug Type	Purpose	Brand Name
Diuretic	Diuretics eliminate excess fluid from the body by increasing urine output.	Hydrodiuril Lasix Enduron Diuril Esidrix Hygroton Bumex Zaroxolyn
Potassium-sparing	Same as diuretics but also reduce excessive loses of potassium.	Aldactone Maxzide Dyazide Dyrenium
Potassium Supplement	Used to counteract loss of potassium from use of diuretics.	K-Dur K-Tab K-Lor Slow-K K-Lyte K-Lyte/Cl Micro-K Micro-KLS Klotrix Kaon
Beta Blocker	Slow the heartbeat, decrease the amount of blood pumped by the heart & dilate the major blood vessels.	Inderal Corgard Tenormin Lopressor Visken Blocadren

Drug Type	Purpose	Brand Name
Vasodilator	Relax muscles responsible for constricting blood vessels. Prescribed in combination with other antihypertensive drugs such as diuretics or beta blockers.	Apresoline Loniten Minipress
Sympathetic Blocker	Block action of epinephrine & norepinephrine. Results in less constricting of blood vessels and decreased heart rate.	Catapres Wytensin Aldomet Tenex Hytrin
Rauwolfia Derivative	Appear to lower blood pressure by decreasing resistance within blood vessels, making it easier for heart to pump blood.	Raudixin Serpasil
ACE Inhibitor	Prevent hormones from converting to other hormones or enzymes that regulate blood pressure.	Capoten Vasotec Zestril. Prinivil
Calcium Channel Blocker	Hinders the entry of calcium into the muscle cells of blood vessels. Prevents the vessels from constricting.	Cardizem Procardia Calan Isoptin

SODIUM

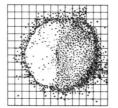

SODIUM'S IMPORTANCE IN HYPERTENSION

For most people, a diet high in sodium isn't a problem – the kidneys just get rid of the extra amounts in the urine. However, when some people eat too much sodium, the kidneys can't get rid of the extra amounts. Levels of sodium rise in the blood and tissues, resulting in hypertension.

Sodium attracts water. (Remember how salt in the salt shaker draws water from the air when it rains and becomes difficult to shake?) If there is more sodium in the blood and tissues there will also be more water. When water increases in body tissues, *edema* – a swelling that occurs especially in the hands, ankles and legs – results.

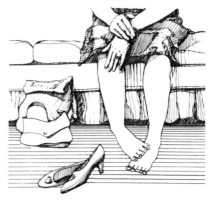
Edema

When there is extra water in the blood, the heart has to work harder to push the extra volume of fluids through the vessels. The work load of the heart is increased and a higher blood pressure may result.

To help get rid of extra water and sodium your physician may prescribe a *diuretic*. Diuretics get rid of extra water by causing the kidneys to increase the urine they produce. When you increase the production of urine, sodium – because it is attracted to the water – is also lost.

TABLE SALT

Another way to reduce water retention is by lowering the sodium or table salt in your diet.

1 tsp. of salt = 2,000 mg

Table salt is a mixture of two minerals – sodium and chloride. Salt is 40 percent sodium and 60 percent chloride. One teaspoon of salt contains about 2,000 mg of sodium. <u>Physicians</u> <u>usually</u> <u>recommend</u> <u>that</u> <u>hypertensive individuals</u> <u>consume</u> <u>no</u> <u>more</u> <u>than</u> <u>2,000</u> <u>mg</u> <u>of</u> <u>sodium</u> <u>daily</u>. This one teaspoon of salt includes natural, table, and processed sources.

DIETARY SODIUM

There are three major sources of sodium in our diet:

1. Sodium is found **naturally** in all foods. Some foods, such as milk, carrots, and celery, naturally have more sodium than other foods. However, unless your sodium intake is severely restricted (less than 1,000 mg per day), it is not necessary to exclude these foods from your diet.

2. About one-third of the salt in our diet comes from the **salt shaker** on our table and the salt that we put in our food as we cook. To reduce salt when you cook:

   • **cut down on salt used in recipes that don't contain yeast.** Adapting to the flavor of low-salt recipes may be easier if salt is first reduced by one-half, then by three-fourths.

   • **change the preparation or cooking method.** You don't need to add salt to water when cooking pasta, vegetables, or cereals. And, you can prepare many foods such as puddings, muffins, and soups from "scratch". It takes very little extra time, and homemade products have much less salt than processed food.

- **substitute ingredients.** Instead of adding salt to your foods when cooking, learn to cook with spices. There are many no-salt spice alternatives. A list of spice blends can be found on page 21. Garlic and celery powder should be used instead of garlic and celery salt. Low-salt or no-salt meat tenderizers and bouillon cubes are also available. Use low-salt or no-salt-added canned foods and low-salt or no-salt-added cheeses in casseroles and other dishes such as lasagna and macaroni and cheese.

To reduce salt at the table:

- **decrease salt slowly at first;** by one-fourth, one-half, then three-fourths. It takes time for your taste buds to adjust – allow four to six weeks .

- **taste before salting!** Many people salt their food out of habit and fail to taste first. Taste, then think, "do I really need to salt this food?" Reach for a spice as an alternative.

- **avoid "extras" that are high in salt,** like catsup, soy sauce, and Worcestershire sauce. Substitute homemade catsup, home prepared mustard, lemon juice, or vinegar.

3. The largest amount of sodium in our diet comes from **processed foods** such as baked goods, canned, pickled, and smoked foods. Manufacturers use sodium to:

    - **preserve and protect** foods such as meats, olives, and salad dressings from bacteria.

    - **enhance the flavor** of breads, cheeses, vegetables, sauces, etc.

    - **develop color** in meat products such as ham, bacon, and hot dogs.

    - **bind or hold together** different types of meats or cheeses with moisture and fat. Processed cheeses and lunch meats are examples of products which use sodium as a binder.

- **ferment** pickles, cheeses, and yeast breads. In cheeses, sodium is used to draw the whey out of the curd. Therefore, softer natural cheeses have less sodium than harder cheeses. In yeast products, sodium controls the action of yeast. In non-yeast baked goods, sodium bicarbonate (baking soda) is used to create gas that makes the product rise.

Take a look at the chart on page 22 and notice the difference processing makes in sodium content. For example, there is only a small amount of sodium in three ounces of plain beef. Process it into dried beef – adding sodium for color, flavor, and as a preservative – and you have a very high-sodium product!

Many homemade recipes in this section are compared to similar processed products to help you see the differences in sodium content. Remember that 1 teaspoon of salt equals a little more than 2,000 mg of sodium. Thus, when 1/2 cup of canned spaghetti sauce contains 925 mg of sodium (almost 1/2 teaspoon of salt) you are better off either making your own sauce or buying an unsalted product. Then, add a small amount of salt and/or spices. Now **you** control the product's salt content! As you adjust to lower sodium recipes, you will enjoy the taste of the food itself more and be annoyed with foods that will seem too salty.

REDUCED-SODIUM PRODUCTS

Many food companies have taken out or reduced the salt in formerly high-salt products. A partial list of such products that may be found in your grocery store follows. Be sure to ask the manager of your grocery store for new reduced-sodium products.

Beverages

vegetable juice - no salt added

tomato juice - no salt added

Breads

taco shells - no salt added

matzo - no salt added

tortilla chips - no salt added

breads - no salt added

wheat, cheese & saltine crackers - low salt or no salt added

Cereals

oatmeal - no salt added

cream of wheat & rice - no salt added

shredded wheat - no salt added

puffed wheat & rice - no salt added

rice cakes - no salt added

frozen & boxed potatoes - no salt added

Condiments/Spices/Dressings

instant beef & chicken broth and marinades - no salt added

soy sauce - low salt*

catsup - low salt* or no salt added

spices - no salt added

meat tenderizer - no salt added

salad dressings - low salt

pickles - low salt

* These products are still high in salt so use sparingly!

Dairy Foods
   swiss, colby & cheddar cheese - low salt or no salt added

   margarine/butter - no salt added

Meat/Protein Foods
   nuts - no salt added

   peanut butter - low salt or no salt added

   white & light tuna - low salt

Sauces/Soups
   spaghetti sauce - no salt added

   soups - low salt or no salt added

   canned tomatoes, purée & sauces - no salt added

Snacks/Sweets
   potato chips - low salt or no salt added

   pretzels - no salt added

   popcorn, microwave - no salt added

Vegetables
   canned corn, green beans, peas, mixed vegetables - no salt
   added

Sodium Definitions on Labels

Reduced sodium - usual sodium level reduced by 75 percent.

Low sodium - 140 mg or less per serving.

Very low sodium - 35 mg or less per serving.

Sodium free - less than five mg per serving.

Unsalted - a normally salted food processed without salt.

Spice Blends

Spices can be used on meats and vegetables instead of salt. Experiment with different spice blends until you find one you like. Begin by adding 1/4 teaspoon for each four servings. Cut back if you find them too strong! Spice blends can also be purchased at your supermarket.

Shaker #1

1-1/2 tsp. thyme

1-1/2 tsp. sage

2 tsp. rosemary

2 tsp. marjoram

2-1/2 tsp. savory

Shaker #2

1 tsp. celery seed

2-1/2 tsp. marjoram

2-1/2 tsp. savory

1-1/2 tsp. thyme

1-1/2 tsp. basil

Shaker #3

2-1/2 tsp. paprika

2-1/2 tsp. garlic powder

2-1/2 tsp. dry mustard

5 tsp. onion powder

1/2 tsp. pepper

1/4 tsp. celery seed

1/2 tsp. parsley flakes

Shaker #4

2 Tbsp. crushed savory

1 Tbsp. dry mustard

2-1/2 tsp. onion powder

1-1/2 tsp. curry powder

1-1/2 tsp. white pepper

1 tsp. ground cumin

1/2 tsp. garlic powder

Shaker #5

2 Tbsp. dillweed or crushed basil leaves

1 tsp. crushed oregano leaves

2 Tbsp. onion powder

1 tsp. celery seed

1/4 tsp. dried grated lemon peel

SODIUM CONTENT OF FOOD

(Recommended – Less Than 2,000 mg)

Food	Amount	Sodium (mg)
MEAT GROUP		
Beef		
cooked & lean	3 oz.	55
corned	3 oz.	802
chipped	3 oz.	3,657
Pork		
fresh, cooked	3 oz.	59
bacon	2 slices	274
ham	3 oz.	1,114
Chicken		
roasted	1 drumstick	47
chicken spread	3 oz.	345
pot pie	1 pie	907
Lunch meats		
bologna, beef	1 slice	220
sausage, pork	1 link	168
hot dog, beef	1	639
VEGETABLE & FRUIT GROUP		
Green Beans - cooked		
fresh	1 cup	5
frozen	1 cup	7
canned	1 cup	326
Lima Beans - cooked		
fresh	1 cup	2
frozen	1 cup	128
canned	1 cup	456

Food	Amount	Sodium (mg)
MILK GROUP		
Skim milk	1 cup	122
Buttermilk	1 cup	257
Yogurt - lowfat, plain	1 cup	159
Ice cream - vanilla	1 cup	112
Cheese		
cottage	1/2 cup	457
swiss	1 oz.	74
cheddar	1 oz.	176
processed American	1 oz.	406
Parmesan	1 oz.	454
BREAD & CEREAL GROUP		
White bread	1 slice	114
Wheat bread	1 slice	132
English muffin	1 medium	293
Stuffing mix (cooked)	1 cup	1,131
Bagel	1	245
Cereals		
grits, regular	3/4 cup	0
grits, instant	3/4 cup	354
oatmeal, regular	3/4 cup	1
oatmeal, quick with		
raisin & spices	3/4 cup	223
Shredded Wheat	1 biscuit	3
Raisin Bran	1/2 cup	209
Corn Flakes	1 cup	256
Rice Krispies	1 cup	340
Crackers		
saltine	2 crackers	70
graham	1 cracker	48

Food	Amount	Sodium (mg)
CONVENIENCE FOODS		
Cake from mix		
yellow	1/12 cake	242
chocolate	1/12 cake	402
Condiments		
Italian dressing	1 Tbsp.	116
French dressing	1 Tbsp.	214
mayonnaise	1 Tbsp.	78
catsup	1 Tbsp.	156
soy sauce	1 Tbsp.	1,029
Worcestershire sauce	1 tsp.	69
garlic powder	1 tsp.	1
garlic salt	1 tsp.	1,850
meat tenderizer	1 tsp.	1,750
olives, green	4	323
pickle, dill	1 large	928
pickle, sweet	1 large	128
Pudding		
home recipe	1/2 cup	73
regular	1/2 cup	195
instant	1/2 cup	470
Soups - canned		
vegetable	1 cup	823
tomato (with water)	1 cup	872
mushroom (with milk)	1 cup	1,076
chicken noodle	1 cup	1,107
Snacks		
potato chips	10 chips	200
pretzels (twist)	1 pretzel	101

MUSTARD

INGREDIENTS IN HOMEMADE RECIPE

1 tsp. dry mustard

1 Tbsp. vinegar

PREPARATION

1. Mix ingredients together and serve. Makes 1 Tbsp.

NUTRIENTS IN 1 TBSP.

	Bottled	Homemade
Calories	15	11
Fat	trace	trace
Carbohydrate	trace	1
Cholesterol	0	0
Potassium	21	26
Calcium	12	6
Sodium	195	trace

CATSUP

INGREDIENTS IN HOMEMADE RECIPE

1 cup no-salt-added tomato purée

1/8 tsp. allspice

1 Tbsp. lemon juice or vinegar

1 Tbsp. sugar

1/4 tsp. dry mustard

PREPARATION

1. Combine all ingredients and cook over low heat for 10 minutes. Store in tightly covered jar in refrigerator. Makes about 1 cup.

NUTRIENTS IN 1 TBSP.

	Bottled	Homemade
Calories	15	10
Fat	trace	0
Carbohydrate	4	2
Cholesterol	0	0
Potassium	54	67
Calcium	3	3
Sodium	156	3

BARBECUE SAUCE

INGREDIENTS IN HOMEMADE RECIPE

1-1/2 cups water

1-1/2 cups low-salt catsup

2-1/2 Tbsp. Worcestershire sauce

5 Tbsp. brown sugar

2/3 cup cider vinegar

PREPARATION

1. Combine all ingredients in a large saucepan. Bring to a boil.

2. Cover pan and simmer gently for about 1-1/2 hours until sauce thickens. Store in tightly covered jar in refrigerator. Makes about 2 cups sauce.

NUTRIENTS IN 1 TBSP.

	Bottled	Homemade
Calories	14	15
Fat	1	0
Carbohydrate	1	4
Cholesterol	0	0
Potassium	27	62
Calcium	3	9
Sodium	130	80

BISCUITS

INGREDIENTS

2 cups flour

1/4 tsp. salt

2-1/2 tsp. baking powder

4 Tbsp. vegetable oil

2/3 cup skim or 1% milk
(1 cup for drop biscuits)

PREPARATION

1. Combine flour, salt, and baking powder in small bowl.

2. Combine milk and oil. Pour all at once into flour mixture. Stir with fork until mixture leaves side of bowl and forms a ball. Remove dough from bowl and knead about 10 times.

3. Roll out dough 1/2" thick. Cut with biscuit cutter or with the top (floured) rim of a glass. Place on an ungreased cookie sheet. Bake 10 to 12 minutes at 475°. Makes 12 biscuits.

NUTRIENTS IN 1 BISCUIT

Calories	121
Fat	5
Carbohydrate	17
Cholesterol	trace
Potassium	43
Calcium	32
Sodium	118

Boxed biscuit mixes can contain more than 270 mg. of sodium in 1 biscuit.

═ CORNBREAD MUFFINS ═

INGREDIENTS IN HOMEMADE RECIPE

1 cup all-purpose flour	1 cup yellow cornmeal
1/4 cup sugar	1 cup skim or 1% milk
2 tsp. baking powder	1 egg
1/4 tsp. salt	2 Tbsp. margarine

PREPARATION

1. Mix together the flour, sugar, baking powder, salt, and cornmeal. In a separate bowl, combine the milk, slightly beaten egg, and melted margarine.

2. Make a well in center of dry ingredients. Pour in liquid ingredients. Stir just until dry ingredients are moistened. Batter will be lumpy. Coat muffin pan with cooking spray. Fill about 3/4 full. Bake 12 to 15 minutes at 350° until lightly browned. Makes 16 muffins.

NUTRIENTS IN 1 MUFFIN

	Boxed Mix	Homemade
Calories	130	95
Fat	4	2
Carbohydrate	20	17
Cholesterol	NA*	17
Potassium	44	49
Calcium	96	30
Sodium	315	101

*NA = not available

BANANA BREAD

INGREDIENTS

1-3/4 cups all-purpose flour

1/2 cup sugar

2 tsp. baking powder

1 tsp. baking soda

1/4 cup wheat germ

1/3 cup plain lowfat yogurt

1 egg plus 3 egg whites

1/4 cup vegetable oil

3 ripe bananas, mashed

PREPARATION

1. Combine flour, sugar, baking powder, and baking soda together. Mix in wheat germ.

2. Add all remaining ingredients and mix until well blended.

3. Pour batter into a 8 x 4" loaf pan coated with cooking spray. Bake for about 1 hour at 350° until toothpick inserted in center comes out clean. Makes sixteen 1/2" slices.

NUTRIENTS IN 1/2 " SLICE

Calories	141
Fat	4
Carbohydrate	23
Cholesterol	17
Potassium	142
Calcium	23
Sodium	111

CORN PUDDING

INGREDIENTS

2 cups fresh or frozen corn

3/4 cup skim or 1% milk

1 egg white

1 egg, slightly beaten

4 tsp. sugar

1 Tbsp. flour

2 Tbsp. margarine, melted

Pepper as desired

PREPARATION

1. Purée 1/4 cup of corn and the milk in a food processor or blender. Pour into a small mixing bowl.

2. Mix in rest of corn and remaining ingredients. Pour into a 1 quart baking dish.

3. Bake, uncovered, at 350° for about 40 minutes or until firm as a custard. Makes 3 cups.

NUTRIENTS IN 1/2 CUP

Calories	115
Fat	5
Carbohydrate	16
Cholesterol	46
Potassium	147
Calcium	46
Sodium	83

Frozen corn pudding can contain over 500 mg of sodium in 1/2 cup!

LEMON VEGETABLES

INGREDIENTS IN HOMEMADE RECIPE

1/2 cup lima beans

1/2 cup sliced carrots

1/2 green pepper, sliced

1 cup sliced yellow
   squash or zucchini

2 tsp. margarine

2 tsp. lemon juice

Pepper as desired

PREPARATION

1. Steam carrots and lima beans in steamer for 5 minutes. Add green pepper and squash. Steam for another 5 minutes.

2. Place in serving dish. Add margarine and lemon juice. Makes 2-1/2 cups.

NUTRIENTS IN 1/2 CUP

	Frozen Commercial	Homemade
Calories	77	48
Fat	3	2
Carbohydrate	9	7
Cholesterol	NA*	0
Potassium	144	218
Calcium	27	19
Sodium	419	25

*NA = not available

MUSHROOM SOUP

INGREDIENTS IN HOMEMADE RECIPE

8 oz. fresh mushrooms

1 small onion, chopped

3 Tbsp. margarine

4 Tbsp. flour

1/4 tsp. salt

Pepper to taste

4 cups skim or 1% milk

PREPARATION

1. Sauté mushrooms and onion just until tender. Do not drain.

2. Melt margarine in medium saucepan. Stir in flour. Let mixture cook over medium heat about 1 min. Remove pan from heat.

3. Add milk SLOWLY to flour mixture. Cook over low heat, stirring constantly, until mixture is slightly thickened.

4. Add mushrooms, salt, pepper, and onions. Makes 4-1/2 cups.

NUTRIENTS IN 1 CUP

	Canned	Homemade
Calories	215	185
Fat	14	8
Carbohydrate	16	19
Cholesterol	NA*	4
Potassium	279	573
Calcium	191	278
Sodium	1076	310

*NA = not available

TURKEY POT PIE

INGREDIENTS IN HOMEMADE RECIPE

Pastry:

> 1/4 cup vegetable oil
>
> 2 Tbsp. water
>
> 1 cup flour

Filling:

> 1/2 cup boiling water
>
> 1/3 cup sliced carrots
>
> 1/3 cup fresh or frozen peas
>
> 1/4 cup diced celery
>
> 1/4 cup chopped onion
>
> 1/3 cup diced potatoes
>
> 2 Tbsp. margarine
>
> 1/4 cup flour

> Pepper to taste
>
> 1/4 tsp. poultry seasoning
>
> 1/4 tsp. salt
>
> 1-1/3 cups homemade chicken broth (or low-salt bouillon)
>
> 2/3 cup skim or 1% milk
>
> 1-1/2 cups diced turkey

PREPARATION

1. To make pastry: Add vegetable oil and water to flour. Mix with fork until dough pulls from side of bowl and forms a ball. Divide into four pieces.

2. Roll each piece of dough between two pieces of wax paper until the dough is 1/2 " wider than the baking dish.

3. To make the filling: Cover and simmer vegetables in water just until tender. Drain.

4. In separate saucepan, melt margarine. Stir in flour and seasonings. Slowly add the broth and milk, stirring constantly until the mixture thickens.

34

5. Add vegetables and turkey. Line four 1 cup baking dishes with dough. Fill with mixture.

6. Put pastry dough over each baking dish. Flute edges of dough with fingers. Cut several slits in top of dough.

7. Bake at 400° about 40 minutes until crust is brown and filling is bubbly. Serves 4.

NUTRIENTS IN 1 CUP

	Frozen Commercial	Homemade
Calories	423	452
Fat	23	22
Carbohydrate	40	39
Cholesterol	NA*	41
Potassium	18	412
Calcium	64	87
Sodium	929	280

*NA=not available

CHILI

INGREDIENTS IN HOMEMADE RECIPE

1/2 lb. lean ground beef

1 garlic clove, crushed

1 small onion, diced

1/4 tsp. salt

1/2 tsp. oregano

1-1/2 tsp. chili powder

6 oz. can no-salt-added
   tomato paste

1-1/2 cups cooked kidney
   or pinto beans

1 cup water

PREPARATION

1. Cook ground beef in nonstick skillet. Add garlic, onion, salt, oregano, and chili powder.

2. Add tomato paste, beans, and water. Mix well. Cover and cook until mixture thickens. Serve over rice. Makes 4 cups.

NUTRIENTS IN 1 CUP

	Canned	Homemade
Calories	340	257
Fat	16	10
Carbohydrate	31	22
Cholesterol	NA*	47
Potassium	594	617
Calcium	82	30
Sodium	1194	203

*NA=not available

SPAGHETTI SAUCE

INGREDIENTS IN HOMEMADE RECIPE

1/3 cup chopped onion

1 minced garlic clove

2 Tbsp. olive oil

1 tsp. Italian seasoning

1 cup water

1 tsp. basil

1 Tbsp. minced parsley

1 tsp. salt

2 tsp. sugar

Pepper to taste

27 oz. can (about 3-1/2 cups) no-salt-added tomatoes

6 oz. can no-salt-added tomato paste

8 oz. can no-salt-added tomato sauce

PREPARATION

1. Cook onion, garlic, and oil slowly in saucepan until tender.
2. Combine all ingredients in a large saucepan. Cover, simmer over low heat for at least 1 hour. Makes 5 cups.

NUTRIENTS IN 1/2 CUP

	Canned	Homemade
Calories	96	70
Fat	4	3
Carbohydrate	14	11
Cholesterol	0	0
Potassium	413	459
Calcium	19	38
Sodium	648	222

LASAGNA

INGREDIENTS IN HOMEMADE RECIPE

1 medium onion, chopped

1/2 lb. lean ground beef

1 clove garlic, minced

15 oz. can no-salt-added tomatoes

2-8 oz. cans no-salt-added tomato sauce

2 tsp. Italian seasoning

1 Tbsp. parsley flakes

1/2 cup fresh chopped mushrooms

1/2 tsp. pepper

1/2 tsp. salt

2 tsp. sugar

2 cups low-fat cottage cheese

1 egg

8 ozs. part-skim mozzarella cheese, shredded

1/2 lb. lasagna noodles (about 10 noodles)

PREPARATION

1. Cook in large saucepan, onion, ground beef, and garlic until tender. Drain off fat.

2. Add tomatoes, sauce, Italian seasoning, parsley flakes, mushrooms, pepper, salt, and sugar. Simmer, stirring occasionally, for 25 minutes until mixture thickens.

3. Cook lasagna noodles according to directions. Drain.

4. Mix together cottage cheese, egg, and mozzarella cheese. Save 2 oz. of mozzarella to sprinkle on top.

5. Coat 8" by 12" baking dish with non-stick spray and layer as follows:

   1 cup sauce

   1/2 noodles

   1/2 cheese

   1/2 remaining sauce mixture

   Remaining noodles

   Remaining cheese

   Remaining sauce

6. Bake at 350° for 35 minutes. Sprinkle remaining cheese on top and bake 10 minutes more. Let stand 10 minutes before serving. For better flavor, make the day before, refrigerate overnight and bake the next day. Serves 8.

NUTRIENTS IN 1 CUP

	Frozen Commercial	Homemade
Calories	344	272
Fat	15	11
Carbohydrate	34	18
Cholesterol	NA*	85
Potassium	476	328
Calcium	363	246
Sodium	835	538

*NA=not available

MEATBALLS

INGREDIENTS

1/4 cup skim or 1% milk

1 egg white

1 small onion, chopped finely

1-1/2 bread slices

3/4 lb. lean ground beef

PREPARATION

1. Combine milk, egg, and onion in mixing bowl. Remove crust from bread, crumble and add to mixture. Add meat and mix thoroughly.

2. Shape into 1" balls. Bake on cookie sheet at 375° for 20-30 minutes. Makes about 24 meatballs.

NUTRIENTS IN 4 MEATBALLS

Calories	170
Fat	9
Carbohydrate	4
Cholesterol	48
Potassium	216
Calcium	27
Sodium	85

VANILLA PUDDING

INGREDIENTS IN HOMEMADE RECIPE

1/3 cup sugar

1/4 cup flour

2 cups skim or 1% milk

1 egg, slightly beaten

1 tsp. vanilla

PREPARATION

1. Mix sugar and flour in medium saucepan.

2. Add the milk gradually to avoid lumps. Cook over medium heat, stirring constantly until mixture thickens.

3. Add a small amount of hot mixture to egg, then add to rest of mixture. Remove from heat and add vanilla. Mixture will thicken as it cools. Makes 2-1/2 cups.

NUTRIENTS IN 1/2 CUP

	Boxed Instant	Homemade
Calories	141	120
Fat	2	1
Carbohydrate	28	22
Cholesterol	NA*	56
Potassium	135	181
Calcium	104	127
Sodium	402	64

*NA = not available

POTASSIUM

POTASSIUM'S IMPORTANCE IN HYPERTENSION

Potassium, another mineral important to hypertensive individuals, is necessary for nerves and muscles to function properly. Along with sodium, potassium maintains water balance. Potassium is found primarily inside the cells in our body – sodium outside the cells. Thus, when diuretics are prescribed by your physician to get rid of sodium, potassium is also lost. How this happens is illustrated in figures 1-3. Normally, there is a "balance" between sodium and potassium in our cells. This balance is shown in figure 1. However, when diuretics flush out excess sodium from the outer cell, the particles are no longer balanced as seen in figure 2. Figure 3, shows potassium inside the cell has moved out to balance the minerals. Both sodium and potassium are then lost in the urine.

To make up for the potassium lost, physicians usually prescribe potassium supplements and/or suggest that their patients eat foods containing lots of potassium. Occasionally, *"potassium-sparing"* diuretics may

Potassium ▼   Sodium ⬡

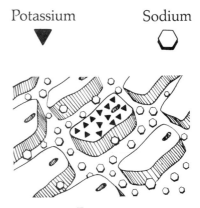

Figure 1
Sodium & Potassium in Balance

Figure 2
Sodium Loss From Outside Cell

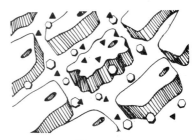

Figure 3
Potassium Moves Out of Cell

be prescribed. These are diuretics that contain potassium. Potassium-sparing diuretics, however, may not be as effective in lowering blood pressure.

DIETARY POTASSIUM

Many people being treated for hypertension don't consume enough potassium in their diets. Fruits, vegetables, milk, and meats are the best sources of potassium. Bananas contain a lot of potassium but there are other fruits and vegetables – some even better sources! Select your favorite potassium sources on page 47 and incorporate them into your diet often. Consuming two to three low-fat, milk sources and at least five fruits and vegetables daily is recommended to obtain enough potassium to meet your needs.

The estimated minimum requirement of potassium is 2,000 mg a day. A hypertensive individual should try to get even more.

The more a food is processed (potassium dissolves in water) the less potassium is available for you to eat. Canned foods are usually not as high in potassium as fresh foods. Thus, try to eat vegetables and fruits raw or cook them in their skins to increase the amount of potassium in your diet.

Some salt substitutes contain large amounts of potassium. The use of salt substitutes containing potassium chloride or any potassium should be checked with your physician. Too much potassium can be as dangerous as too little!

POTASSIUM CONTENT OF COMMON FOODS
(Recommended - more than 2,000 mg a day)

Food	Amount	Calories	Potassium(mg)
Milk Group -			
yogurt, plain	1 cup	145	531
skim	1 cup	85	406
whole	1 cup	150	370
Fruit/Vegetable Group -			
potato, baked	1 med.	145	782
cantaloupe	1/2 (5")	80	682
potato, boiled	1 med.	105	556
orange juice	1 cup	120	503
squash, winter	1/2 cup	65	473
banana	1 med.	100	440
beans, lima	1/2 cup	85	362
tomato	1 med.	25	300
prune, dried	5 large	110	298
orange	1 med.	65	263
dates	5	110	259
carrot	1 med.	30	246
collards, frozen	1/2 cup	25	201
broccoli	1/2 cup	25	196
Meat Group -			
haddock, fried	3 oz.	140	296
hamburger	3 oz.	185	261
turkey	1/2 cup	133	257
chicken, broiled	3 oz.	120	242
pork, roast	3 oz.	310	233
meat substitutes -			
sunflower seeds	1/2 cup	405	667

FROSTED MELON

INGREDIENTS

1/2 cantaloupe, cubed

8 oz. lowfat plain yogurt

10 oz. package frozen strawberries

PREPARATION

1. Chill melon until ready to serve.

2. Combine remaining ingredients into blender or food processor container. Place container in freezer until serving time. When ready to serve, remove from freezer and blend until slushy.

3. Remove melon from refrigerator. Divide into four separate dishes. Pour berry mixture over melon cubes. Serve immediately. Serves 4.

NUTRIENTS IN 1 CUP

Calories	132
Fat	1
Carbohydrate	29
Cholesterol	4
Potassium	448
Calcium	120
Sodium	49

BANANA MILK SHAKE

INGREDIENTS

1 cup sliced ripe banana

1/2 tsp. vanilla

1 cup skim or 1% milk

PREPARATION

1. Combine banana and vanilla in blender or food processor container. Mix until creamy.

2. Add milk and blend until smooth. Chill before serving. Makes 2 cups.

NUTRIENTS IN 1 CUP

Calories	146
Fat	1
Carbohydrate	33
Cholesterol	2
Potassium	651
Calcium	157
Sodium	64

FRUIT SHAKE

INGREDIENTS

1 cup ripe fresh berries such as strawberries or raspberries

1 large banana

3/4 cup apricot or peach nectar

3 ice cubes

PREPARATION

1. Place cut-up fruit in blender or food processor container.

2. Add fruit nectar and ice cubes. Cover container and blend on high about 1 minute until thick and smooth. Serve immediately. Makes 2 cups.

NUTRIENTS IN 1 CUP	
Calories	129
Fat	1
Carbohydrate	33
Cholesterol	0
Potassium	466
Calcium	20
Sodium	2

FRUIT ICES

INGREDIENTS

2 cups puréed fresh fruit such as strawberries

1/4 cup sugar

2 Tbsp. lemon juice

1/2 cup water

PREPARATION

1. Simmer fruit, sugar, and lemon juice in water until soft. Cool.

2. Place mixture in blender or food processor container and purée.

3. Pour mixture into an 8" square pan, cover and freeze. When semi-hard, blend mixture about 1 minute until thick and smooth. Serve immediately. Makes 3 cups.

NUTRIENTS IN 1 CUP

Calories	92
Fat	trace
Carbohydrate	24
Cholesterol	0
Potassium	175
Calcium	15
Sodium	4

MANDARIN GELATIN MOLDS

INGREDIENTS

1 envelope unflavored gelatin

2 cups unsweetened orange juice

2 tsp. sugar

16 oz. can mandarin oranges

2 medium bananas

PREPARATION

1. Sprinkle gelatin over 1/2 cup orange juice and let stand for 1 minute. Add sugar.

2. Boil remaining 1-1/2 cup orange juice. Add to gelatin mixture, stirring until gelatin dissolves.

3. Cool in refrigerator until mixture is consistency of unbeaten egg white. Drain oranges and cut up banana. Add fruit to gelatin mixture. Serves 6.

NUTRIENTS IN 1/2 CUP

Calories	98
Fat	trace
Carbohydrate	24
Cholesterol	0
Potassium	400
Calcium	5
Sodium	14

BAKED BUTTERNUT SQUASH

INGREDIENTS

1 medium butternut squash

2 Tbsp. brown sugar

1 tsp. lemon juice

4 tsp. margarine

PREPARATION

1. Cut squash in half lengthwise, scraping out seeds.

2. Place squash, cup side up, in baking dish. Pour 1/2" water in baking dish.

3. Sprinkle brown sugar and lemon juice on each half. Dot each half with margarine.

4. Cover and bake at 375° for 30 minutes. Uncover and bake 30 more minutes. Serves 4.

NUTRIENTS IN 1/2 SQUASH

Calories	101
Fat	4
Carbohydrate	17
Cholesterol	0
Potassium	318
Calcium	49
Sodium	50

POTATOES-IN-A HALF-SHELL

INGREDIENTS

4 medium baking potatoes

1/2 cup skim or 1% milk

1 Tbsp. margarine

1/4 cup shredded reduced-fat cheddar cheese

PREPARATION

1. Wash and bake potatoes until done. Cool slightly.

2. Cut in half lengthwise and scoop out potato being careful not to break or tear shell.

3. Whip potato with skim milk and margarine until fluffy.

4. Mound back into shells. Bake at 350° for 10 minutes.

5. Sprinkle with cheese and bake 5 minutes more until cheese melts. Serves 8.

NUTRIENTS IN 1/2 POTATO

Calories	101
Fat	2
Carbohydrates	18
Cholesterol	3
Potassium	335
Calcium	48
Sodium	55

═ TUNA-CHEESE POTATO ═

INGREDIENTS

1 med. baking potato

1/4 cup chopped celery

1/4 cup chopped onion

1 tsp. margarine

1/4 cup chopped green pepper

1 (6-1/4 oz.) can low-salt tuna

3 Tbsp. reduced-fat mayonnaise

1/4 cup shredded mozzarella cheese

PREPARATION

1. Bake potato until done. Cool. Cut in half lengthwise. Scoop out potato being careful not to tear skin.

2. Sauté celery, onion, and green pepper in margarine.

3. Mash potato with fork and stir in all remaining ingredients except cheese.

4. Divide mixture into each shell. Bake on cookie sheet 10 minutes at 350°. Remove from oven and sprinkle with cheese. Bake 5 minutes more until cheese melts. Serves 2.

NUTRIENTS IN 1/2 POTATO

Calories	283
Fat	9
Carbohydrates	24
Cholesterol	43
Potassium	652
Calcium	113
Sodium	370

SWISS LIMA BEANS

INGREDIENTS

10 oz. package frozen lima beans (or 1-1/2 cups fresh)

1-1/2 Tbsp. margarine   3 oz. low-fat Swiss cheese, shredded

1-1/2 Tbsp. flour   2 Tbsp. grated onion

1-1/4 cups skim or 1% milk

PREPARATION

1. Cook beans according to package directions. Drain.

2. In medium saucepan, melt margarine. Add flour, stirring constantly. Cook over low heat for one minute.

3. Remove pan from heat and slowly add milk to prevent lumps. Cook over low heat, stirring constantly, until mixture thickens.

4. Remove pan from heat. Add cheese and stir until it melts.

5. Combine beans and onion into a small 1-quart casserole dish. Pour cheese sauce over beans. Bake at 350° for 20 minutes until bubbly. Makes 2-1/2 cups.

NUTRIENTS IN 1/2 CUP

Calories	166
Fat	7
Carbohydrate	15
Cholesterol	13
Potassium	339
Calcium	300
Sodium	131

SPINACH PUFF

INGREDIENTS IN HOMEMADE RECIPE

10 oz. package frozen chopped spinach
    (asparagus, or broccoli)

3 Tbsp. margarine   Pepper to taste
3 Tbsp. flour   1 oz. low-fat
1 cup skim or 1% milk   Swiss cheese,
1 egg plus 1 egg white   shredded

PREPARATION

1. Cook spinach until tender. Drain.
2. Melt margarine in medium saucepan. Add flour. Cook, 1 minute over low heat, stirring constantly. Remove pan from heat and gradually add milk to prevent lumps. Cook over medium heat until thick, stirring constantly.
3. Separate egg yolk from white. Beat yolk until thick. Slowly add a small amount of white sauce into egg yolk. Add sauce and yolk to remaining sauce. Stir in spinach, pepper, and cheese.
4. Beat egg whites until stiff peaks form. Fold whites into spinach mixture. Pour into a casserole dish coated with cooking spray. Bake at 375° for 40 minutes. Serve immediately. Makes 2-1/2 cups.

NUTRIENTS IN 1/2 CUP

	Frozen Commercial	Homemade
Calories	140	149
Fat	8	9
Carbohydrate	12	10
Cholesterol	NA*	60
Potassium	250	300
Calcium	133	229
Sodium	600	192

*NA=not available

APPLE SQUASH

INGREDIENTS

2 medium acorn squash

4 tsp. margarine, melted

1 cup chopped apples

4 Tbsp. maple-flavored syrup

1/2 tsp. ground nutmeg

PREPARATION

1. Cut squash in half lengthwise and scoop out seeds.

2. Place squash cut side down in shallow baking dish. Pour boiling water in about 1" deep. Bake uncovered at 375° for 30 minutes.

3. Turn squash cut side up. Add to each squash half – 1 tsp. margarine, 1/4 cup chopped apples, and 1 Tbsp. syrup. Sprinkle each with nutmeg. Bake squash uncovered at 375° for 30 to 35 more minutes until apples are tender. Serves 4.

NUTRIENTS IN 1/2 SQUASH

Calories	122
Fat	trace
Carbohydrate	31
Cholesterol	0
Potassium	289
Calcium	34
Sodium	17

OVEN FRENCH FRIES

INGREDIENTS

4 medium baking potatoes

1 Tbsp. vegetable oil

PREPARATION

1. Peel (or leave peeling on) and slice potatoes into lengthwise strips about 1/2 " wide. Thoroughly dry on paper towel.

2. Place potatoes into a plastic baggy. Add vegetable oil. Shake bag thoroughly, coating potatoes with oil.

3. Spread potatoes in a single layer on a cookie sheet. Bake at 475° turning occasionally for about 30 minutes or until brown. For extra crispy fries, brown under broiler for a few additional minutes. Serves 8.

NUTRIENTS IN 1/2 POTATO

Calories	88
Fat	2
Carbohydrate	17
Cholesterol	0
Potassium	305
Calcium	4
Sodium	4

Potatoes fried the traditional way can contain over 12 g. of fat in 1/2 cup!

BAKED BEANS

INGREDIENTS IN HOMEMADE RECIPE

1 cup dry navy beans

1/4 cup molasses

1/2 tsp. dry mustard

3 slices bacon, crumbled

1/2 medium onion, diced

1/4 tsp. salt

PREPARATION

1. Rinse beans thoroughly. Cover with water and soak overnight.

2. Rinse beans, add 1 quart of water and simmer, covered, until tender. Drain beans, reserving 1 cup of liquid (add water if necessary to make 1 cup). Add the molasses and dry mustard to the reserved liquid.

3. Combine beans, bacon, salt, and onion in a one-quart casserole dish. Pour liquid over the beans and bake at 300°, covered, for 3 to 4 hours. Makes 3 cups. This recipe can easily be doubled.

NUTRIENTS IN 1/2 CUP

	Canned	Homemade
Calories	155	168
Fat	4	2
Carbohydrate	24	29
Cholesterol	0	3
Potassium	268	548
Calcium	69	74
Sodium	464	140

POTATO SALAD

INGREDIENTS IN LOW-FAT RECIPE

3 pounds potatoes

2 hard-cooked eggs

1/2 cup diced celery

4 green onions, chopped

1/4 cup low-fat mayonnaise

1/4 cup diced green pepper

1/4 cup lowfat plain yogurt

1 tsp. mustard

1 tsp. vinegar

Pepper to taste

1/2 tsp. salt

PREPARATION

1. Boil potatoes in water just until tender – about 20 minutes. Drain and cool. Peel and cut into cubes.

2. Combine remaining ingredients and mix into potatoes. Makes 5 cups.

NUTRIENTS IN 1/2 CUP

	Regular Homemade	Low-Fat Homemade
Calories	144	154
Fat	6	3
Carbohydrate	19	29
Cholesterol	NA*	57
Potassium	389	500
Calcium	35	31
Sodium	628	128

*NA=not available

61

CALCIUM

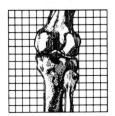

CALCIUM'S IMPORTANCE IN HYPERTENSION

Another mineral important to hypertensive individuals is calcium. Most of the calcium in our bodies is found in the bones and teeth. A very small amount is found in the blood. The calcium in our blood helps to maintain a normal heartbeat and muscle contractions. Calcium continually moves in and out of the bones where it is stored to keep blood levels constant. When dietary calcium is low, calcium is moved out of bone storage to maintain blood levels. When dietary calcium is above the amount needed, it is stored.

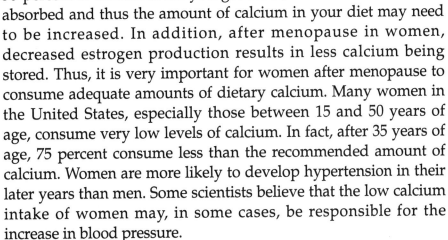

Not all of the calcium that you consume is absorbed. In fact, if you are healthy, only about 30 percent is absorbed. As you get older, less is absorbed and thus the amount of calcium in your diet may need to be increased. In addition, after menopause in women, decreased estrogen production results in less calcium being stored. Thus, it is very important for women after menopause to consume adequate amounts of dietary calcium. Many women in the United States, especially those between 15 and 50 years of age, consume very low levels of calcium. In fact, after 35 years of age, 75 percent consume less than the recommended amount of calcium. Women are more likely to develop hypertension in their later years than men. Some scientists believe that the low calcium intake of women may, in some cases, be responsible for the increase in blood pressure.

Exercise is also important for maintaining calcium absorption. Exercise that puts weight on bones, such as walking and bicycling, increases absorption. However, some medications and foods can interfere with calcium absorption. Diuretics, some antibiotics, caffeine, nicotine, high-fat or high-protein diets, and some vegetables, such as spinach, may **decrease** the amount of calcium absorbed.

DIETARY CALCIUM

The recommended daily dietary allowance of calcium for healthy men and women is 800 mg a day – equal to approximately two and one half calcium sources. Common calcium sources are one cup of milk or yogurt, one ounce of cheese or one and one half cups of cottage cheese or ice cream. When absorption is decreased due to age, inactivity, menopause or illness, dietary calcium should be increased to approximately four calcium sources or 1,200 mg a day.

Most of the calcium in our diet comes from dairy products. Refer to the chart on page 69 for your favorite sources. Remember, the more processed a product the more sodium it contains. For example, processed cheeses, canned soups, and boxed puddings are much higher in sodium than the same product homemade. Whole milk products contain cholesterol and fat that should be limited in a hypertensive's diet. Thus, it is always best to select low-fat milks (skim, 1 percent, or 2 percent), and low-fat cheeses.

Many people have difficulty digesting milk sugar (lactose). An enzyme called lactase which is produced by the body, is needed to break down the milk sugar. When lactose is not broken down, it passes through the digestive system without being digested and absorbed. Symptoms such as gas, cramps, diarrhea, and bloating may develop. A doctor should be seen to diagnose lactose intolerance because these symptoms could also be the signs of other medical conditions. Blacks, Hispanics, Native Americans, and Orientals are most often affected by lactose intolerance. Certain intestinal diseases, some medications, or gastric surgery may also result in temporary or permanent intolerance to lactose.

Some individuals with lactose intolerance may be able to drink a cup of milk without having symptoms. Others may have severe reactions from even very small amounts of milk. A personal tolerance level should be determined.

When milk can be tolerated, small amounts should be consumed with other foods. Even if milk cannot be consumed, yogurt and aged cheeses such as Swiss and cheddar are often tolerated. In addition, lactose-reduced milk and an enzyme-treated milk are available in grocery stores.

Ways to increase calcium in your diet using NONFAT DRY MILK. Add:
- 2 Tbsp. nonfat dry milk to a glass of skim milk or 1 Tbsp. in a glass of orange juice.
- 2 Tbsp. nonfat dry milk to waffle or pancake batters.
- 2 Tbsp. nonfat dry milk to 1 cup of yogurt, hot cereal or mashed potatoes.
- 1/4 cup nonfat dry milk to pudding mixes.
- 1/4 cup nonfat dry milk to cream soups.
- 1/4 cup nonfat dry milk to 1 lb. of hamburger.

Ways to increase calcium in your diet using YOGURT. Plain yogurt makes a good substitute for sour cream in:
- stroganoff.
- baked potatoes.
- dips and vegetable sauces.
- salad dressings.
- baked products.

Ways to increase calcium in your diet using low-fat, part-skim CHEESES. Add cheese to:

- eggs.
- soups such as potato & broccoli.
- sauces over vegetables.
- pizza.
- grits.
- sandwiches.
- casseroles.

Other ways to increase calcium in your diet:

- use yogurt instead of milk with cold cereal.
- make your hot breakfast cereal with milk instead of water.
- use yogurt instead of the 2nd cup of water in gelatin recipes.

CALCIUM CONTENT OF COMMON FOODS
(Recommended - at least 800 mg a day)

Food	Amount	Calories	Calcium (mg)
Yogurt - lowfat plain	1 cup	145	415
fruit flavored	1 cup	230	343
Milk - skim	1 cup	85	302
whole	1 cup	150	291
buttermilk	1 cup	100	285
Cheese - swiss	1 oz.	105	272
mozzarella (skim)	1 oz.	80	207
cheddar	1 oz.	115	204
processed	1 oz.	105	174 *
food	1 oz.	95	163 *
cottage (2% fat)	1 cup	205	155
cream cheese	1 oz.	100	23
Ice Cream - soft	1 cup	375	236
hard	1 cup	270	176
ice milk	1 cup	185	176
Vegetables - cooked			
collards, frozen	1 cup	50	299
kale, frozen	1 cup	40	157
broccoli, fresh	1 cup	40	136
Convenience foods			
pudding, instant	1 cup	325	374 *
macaroni & cheese	1 cup	230	199 *
tomato soup	1 cup	175	168 *
pizza (frozen)	1 sector	145	86 *

* These foods are high in sodium and should be limited or homemade.

STRAWBERRY SMOOTHIE

INGREDIENTS

2 cups vanilla ice milk

1-1/2 cup fresh strawberries

2 tsp. lemon juice

2 cups crushed ice

PREPARATION

1. Combine all ingredients into a blender or food processor container and blend until smooth. Makes 4 cups.

NUTRIENTS IN 1 CUP

Calories	109
Fat	3
Carbohydrate	19
Cholesterol	9
Potassium	227
Calcium	96
Sodium	54

A small fast food shake (about 1 cup) can contain more than 50 g of carbohydrate!

JUICE SHAKE

INGREDIENTS

2 cups cold juice such as orange, grape or pineapple

1/2 cup nonfat dry milk

1/2 tsp. vanilla

1 cup crushed ice

PREPARATION

1. Combine all ingredients into a blender or food processor container. Mix until smooth. Makes 3 cups.

NUTRIENTS IN 1 CUP

Calories	115
Fat	trace
Carbohydrate	24
Cholesterol	2
Potassium	509
Calcium	154
Sodium	63

FRUIT & YOGURT POPSICLE

INGREDIENTS IN HOMEMADE

3 cups sliced strawberries

1/2 cup sugar

1 cup juice from strawberries

1 Tbsp. unflavored gelatin

2 cups plain lowfat yogurt

PREPARATION

1. Add sugar to strawberries. Let stand at room temperature for 30 minutes. Drain strawberries. Add enough water to remaining juice to make 1 cup liquid.

2. Pour liquid into a small saucepan. Stir gelatin into liquid and let stand about 5 minutes. Barely heat the mixture until gelatin dissolves.

3. Combine strawberries, liquid, and yogurt in blender or food processor container. Blend until smooth.

4. Pour about 5 oz. into 12 paper or popsicle cups. Insert sticks and freeze. Serves 12.

NUTRIENTS IN 1 POPSICLE

	Frozen Commercial	Homemade
Calories	70	66
Fat	0	1
Carbohydrate	18	13
Cholesterol	0	2
Potassium	0	157
Calcium	0	74
Sodium	NA*	27

*NA=not available

HOT COCOA

INGREDIENTS IN HOMEMADE RECIPE

4 Tbsp. sugar

1/4 cup unsweetened cocoa

1/3 cup water

4 cups skim or 1% milk

3/4 tsp. vanilla

PREPARATION

1. Combine all ingredients and heat. Makes 4-1/2 cups.

NUTRIENTS IN 1 CUP

	Packaged Instant	Homemade
Calories	100	135
Fat	1	1
Carbohydrate	20	23
Cholesterol	NA*	4
Potassium	227	439
Calcium	167	275
Sodium	232	113

*NA=not available

VEGETABLE-CHEESE SOUP

INGREDIENTS

1/2 cup chopped celery

1/2 cup chopped carrots

1/4 cup chopped onion

1 cup chopped potatoes

1/4 cup margarine

1/4 cup flour

3 cups skim or 1% milk

Pepper to taste

4 oz. reduced-fat cheddar cheese, shredded

PREPARATION

1. Boil vegetables for 5 to 10 minutes in 3/4 cup of water until tender. Do not drain.

2. Melt margarine in medium saucepan and slowly stir in flour. Let mixture cook over medium heat about 1 min.

3. Remove from heat and SLOWLY add milk. Mix well. Cook over medium heat until sauce thickens. Add cooked vegetables to milk and margarine mixture.

4. Remove from heat. Stir in cheese until melted. You may use other vegetables for this soup such as broccoli or turnips. Makes 6 cups.

NUTRIENTS IN 1 CUP

Calories	203
Fat	10
Carbohydrate	21
Cholesterol	9
Potassium	437
Calcium	232
Sodium	234

One cup of canned cheese soup may contain more than 1,000 mg of sodium & 14 g of fat!

CRUSTLESS QUICHE

INGREDIENTS

10 oz. pkg. frozen broccoli spears

3 eggs

1 cup plain lowfat yogurt

3/4 cup evaporated skim milk

2 Tbsp. cornstarch

2 cups shredded low-fat swiss cheese

1 small onion, chopped

1/3 cup chopped celery

1/4 tsp. nutmeg

Pepper to taste

PREPARATION

1. Cook broccoli according to package directions. Drain.
2. Beat eggs with yogurt, evaporated milk, and cornstarch.
3. Stir in remaining ingredients, except broccoli.
4. Coat a 9" round baking pan with cooking spray. Pour cheese mixture into baking pan. Place broccoli spears in spoke-fashion around pan. Bake at 350° for 30 minutes until mixture is set. Serves 6. May substitute spinach, zucchini, etc. for broccoli. Use about 1-1/2 cup.

NUTRIENTS IN 1/6 OF 9" PIE

Calories	234
Fat	10
Carbohydrate	13
Cholesterol	167
Potassium	380
Calcium	670
Sodium	187

MACARONI & CHEESE

INGREDIENTS IN HOMEMADE RECIPE

2 Tbsp. margarine

2 Tbsp. flour

2-1/2 cups skim or 1% milk

1/4 tsp. salt

Pepper to taste

1/2 tsp. dry mustard

2 cups shredded reduced-fat cheddar cheese

2 cups cooked (1 cup uncooked) elbow macaroni

PREPARATION

1. Melt margarine in small saucepan. Add flour stirring until smooth. Remove from heat and slowly add milk to prevent lumps. Add pepper, salt, and mustard. Return to heat. Stir until mixture thickens slightly (for a thin white sauce). Remove from heat. Stir in cheese.

2. Coat a 1-1/2 quart casserole dish with cooking oil spray.

3. Put cooked macaroni into casserole. Pour cheese sauce over macaroni and mix thoroughly. Bake uncovered at 350° for 35 minutes. Makes 4 cups.

NUTRIENTS IN 1 CUP

	Canned	Homemade
Calories	230	239
Fat	10	11
Carbohydrate	26	19
Cholesterol	NA*	28
Potassium	139	240
Calcium	199	400
Sodium	1310	458

*NA=not available

SPINACH CRÊPES

INGREDIENTS

Basic crêpe:

1 whole egg plus 2 extra egg whites

3/4 cup flour

3/4 cup skim or 1% milk

1 Tbsp. vegetable oil

Filling:

10 oz. package frozen chopped spinach

1/2 cup ricotta cheese

3 Tbsp. evaporated skim milk

1 egg white

PREPARATION

1. For crêpes: Slightly beat eggs in bowl. Alternately add milk and flour, beating until smooth. Add oil, stirring until blended. Chill for 1 hour.

2. Cook in crêpe pan or skillet coated with cooking spray, using about 4 Tbsp. batter per crepe. Tip pan to distribute batter thinly. When bottom is browned slightly, turn and brown on other side.

3. For filling: Cook spinach according to package directions. Drain. Add ricotta cheese, milk, and egg. Mix until smooth.

4. Put 2 Tbsp. filling in each crêpe, overlap sides and place in baking dish. Brush with margarine. Bake at 350° for 20 minutes. Makes 8 filled crêpes. Serve crêpes with cheese sauce.

NUTRIENTS IN 1 CRÊPE

Calories	118
Fat	4
Carbohydrate	14
Cholesterol	40
Potassium	227
Calcium	150
Sodium	98

One commercially frozen crêpe can contain 10 g of fat and 600 mg of sodium!

CHEESE SAUCE

INGREDIENTS IN HOMEMADE RECIPE

1 Tbsp. margarine

2 Tbsp. flour

1 cup skim or 1% milk

4 oz. reduced-fat cheddar cheese, shredded

PREPARATION

1. Melt margarine in saucepan until it bubbles.

2. Remove saucepan from heat and add flour. Stir until smooth. Return to heat. Cook 1 minute stirring constantly.

3. Gradually add milk and cook over low heat until thick. Add cheese. Makes 1 cup.

NUTRIENTS IN 2 Tbsp.

	Canned	Homemade
Calories	45	51
Fat	3	3
Carbohydrate	2	3
Cholesterol	8	6
Potassium	27	60
Calcium	88	89
Sodium	248	85

BAKED GRITS & CHEESE

INGREDIENTS

2-1/2 cups skim or 1% milk

3/4 cup regular grits, uncooked

1 Tbsp. margarine

4 oz. reduced-fat cheddar cheese, shredded

PREPARATION

1. Bring milk to a boil and add grits. Cook until thickened, about 10 minutes, stirring often.

2. Add margarine and cheese. Pour into 1 quart baking dish. Bake at 325° for 20 minutes. Serves 8.

NUTRIENTS IN 1/2 CUP

Calories	73
Fat	3
Carbohydrate	7
Cholesterol	6
Potassium	139
Calcium	145
Sodium	108

Instant packets of grits flavored with cheese or bacon contain 450 to 650 mg of sodium in 1 package!

PIZZA

INGREDIENTS

Crust: 1 cup hot water

2 Tbsp. vegetable oil

1/4 tsp. salt

1 package dry yeast

3 to 4 cups flour

Sauce: 2-16 oz. cans no-salt-added tomatoes, chopped

1 small onion, chopped

1 tsp. sugar

1 tsp. oregano

Pepper to taste

2 bay leaves

1/4 tsp. salt

Top: 3/4 lb. lean ground beef

1 cup sliced fresh mushrooms,

2 small green peppers, chopped

10 oz. low-fat mozzarella cheese, shredded

PREPARATION

1. For dough: Boil water and in large mixing bowl combine with oil and salt.

2. When mixture is lukewarm, sprinkle yeast over top. Stir until yeast is dissolved.

3. Gradually add flour, stirring after each addition. Knead dough until smooth and elastic. Shape dough into ball and place in a greased bowl. Turn once to grease top. Cover and let rise in a warm place until doubled-about 1 hour.

4. Punch dough down. Grease hands lightly and shape to fit

pizza pan. Make a 1/2" border around the dough to hold in sauce. Makes about twelve, 2-1/2" slices.

5. For sauce: Combine all sauce ingredients into a medium saucepan. (Don't drain tomatoes.) Cover and let simmer over low heat for 1 hour. Stir occasionally. Remove bay leaves before spreading on crust.

6. For topping: Cook ground beef and drain fat. Sauté green pepper and mushrooms just until tender.

7. Spread ground beef, green pepper, and mushrooms over sauce. Bake pizza at 450° for about 10 minutes.

8. Sprinkle cheese on top of pizza. Return to oven for another 10 minutes until melted and dough edges are slightly browned.

NUTRIENTS IN 2 1/2" SLICE

Calories	291
Fat	11
Carbohydrate	30
Cholesterol	37
Potassium	372
Calcium	187
Sodium	224

CHOCOLATE PUDDING

INGREDIENTS IN HOMEMADE

3 Tbsp. unsweetened cocoa   1/3 cup plus 2 Tbsp. sugar

1-1/2 Tbsp. vegetable oil   2-1/2 cups skim or 1% milk

1/3 cup flour   3/4 tsp. vanilla

PREPARATION

1. Combine cocoa, vegetable oil, flour, and sugar in a medium saucepan. Mix well.

2. Stir milk SLOWLY into dry ingredients to prevent lumps.

3. Cook over medium heat until mixture thickens. Cool and add vanilla. Makes 3 cups.

NUTRIENTS IN 1/2 CUP

	Boxed Mix	Homemade
Calories	163	158
Fat	4	4
Carbohydrate	32	26
Cholesterol	NA*	2
Potassium	168	228
Calcium	187	131
Sodium	470	57

*NA=not available

TAPIOCA PUDDING

INGREDIENTS IN HOMEMADE RECIPE

3 egg whites

1-2/3 cups skim or 1% milk

4 Tbsp. sugar

2 Tbsp. quick-cooking tapioca

1/8 tsp. salt

1-1/2 tsp. vanilla

PREPARATION

1. Combine egg whites and milk in a large saucepan.

2. Add sugar, salt and tapioca.

3. Cook over medium heat, stirring constantly, until mixture comes to a boil. Remove from heat. Cool and add vanilla. Makes 2 cups.

NUTRIENTS IN 1/2 CUP

	Boxed Mix	Homemade
Calories	160	109
Fat	4	trace
Carbohydrate	27	21
Cholesterol	17	2
Potassium	186	203
Calcium	147	129
Sodium	170	90

BAKED CUSTARD

INGREDIENTS IN HOMEMADE RECIPE

1 egg   1 tsp. vanilla

1 cup skim or 1% milk   2 tsp. sugar

Nutmeg

PREPARATION

1. Beat egg slightly in medium bowl.

2. Add all remaining ingredients and beat well.

3. Rinse custard cups with cold water to prevent sticking. Pour mixture into cups then place cups in shallow pan of water. Sprinkle with nutmeg. Bake at 350° until knife inserted in center comes out clean — about 45 minutes. Makes 1 cup.

NUTRIENTS IN 1/2 CUP

	Boxed Mix	Homemade
Calories	153	98
Fat	8	3
Carbohydrate	15	10
Cholesterol	NA*	139
Potassium	194	235
Calcium	149	165
Sodium	209	98

*NA=not available

FATS

It's no surprise that we are confused about the kind of fat we should and shouldn't eat. TV ads tell us cholesterol is bad and that unsaturated fats are good. Physicians tell us cholesterol and triglyceride levels are up. Just what is a fat and which ones should we be concerned about?

FATS: A DEFINITION

We need fat to carry fat-soluble vitamins in our body, to protect organs, to insulate us from heat and cold, and to provide energy. But, fats contain more than twice as many calories as carbohydrates or protein of equal weight and they can be stored efficiently by the body so it is important to keep track of how much fat you consume. Fats important in the control of high blood pressure are:

- *triglycerides.* Dietary fats, after being broken down by the body, appear in the blood mainly as triglycerides. If more fat is consumed than the body is able to use, the excess is stored in cells specifically designed for the job. While waiting to be absorbed by fat cells or used as energy, excess fat in the form of triglycerides may be circulating in the blood stream. Also, when too many simple carbohydrates such as table sugar, sweets, and pop are eaten, they can also be converted to triglycerides.

- *cholesterol.* Cholesterol is a fat-like waxy substance found in every cell of our body. Cholesterol is the major substance in brain tissue. It surrounds the nerve fibers, is important in maintaining strong cell membranes, and is necessary to manufacture important hormones in our body such as vitamin D and sex hormones. The body can make all the cholesterol it needs. However, we get additional cholesterol from the animal foods that we eat. Normally a balance is maintained between what we eat and what our body makes. If we eat a lot, the body makes less. If we didn't eat any, our body would make the needed amount.

Cholesterol is found only in animal products. Don't let food companies fool you. Cooking oils and margarines labeled NO CHOLESTEROL never did contain cholesterol because they are made from the oils of vegetable plants such as sunflower, corn, and soybeans. Butter, milk, and cheeses (as well as meats) do have cholesterol because they are animal foods.

- *saturated and unsaturated.* Saturated and unsaturated simply refers to the chemical structure of a fat (triglyceride). Saturated fats are firm and solid at room temperature. Animal fats such as butter and lard contain mostly saturated fats. Unsaturated fats (liquid at room temperature) are mostly in vegetable foods such as sunflower seed or corn oil. **Palm oil and coconut oils are an exception and should be avoided; they contain highly saturated fats and will raise the level of cholesterol in the body.**

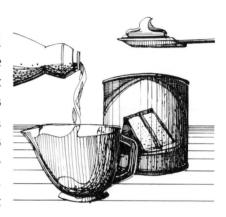

Saturated and Polyunsaturated Content of Fats & Oils		
Food	Saturated(%)	Polyunsaturated(%)
Canola Oil	6	94
Safflower Oil	9	91
Corn Oil	13	87
Olive Oil	14	86
Peanut Oil	18	82
Margarine (stick)	20	80
Lard	41	59
Butter	66	34
Palm Kernel Oil	86	14
Coconut Oil	92	8

Research has shown that a special kind of unsaturated fat found in fish, called *omega-3 fats,* may help to lower blood pressure and prevent heart disease. For this reason, it is recommended that a fish source be included at least twice a week in your diet. Cold water fish such as salmon and tuna have more omega-3 fats than other types of fish.

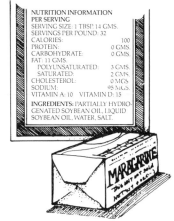

NUTRITION INFORMATION
PER SERVING
SERVING SIZE: 1 TBSP. 14 GMS.
SERVINGS PER POUND: 32
CALORIES: 100
PROTEIN: 0 GMS.
CARBOHYDRATE: 0 GMS.
FAT: 11 GMS.
  POLYUNSATURATED: 3 GMS.
  SATURATED: 2 GMS
CHOLESTEROL: 0 MGS
SODIUM: 95 MGS.
VITAMIN A: 10 VITAMIN D: 15
INGREDIENTS: PARTIALLY HYDRO-
GENATED SOYBEAN OIL, LIQUID
SOYBEAN OIL, WATER, SALT.

Hydrogenation is a process that causes an unsaturated fat to become more saturated. A hydrogenated product is therefore more saturated and less desirable than an unsaturated product. Food companies hydrogenate a food to make a liquid solid at room temperature and to give it a longer shelf life. Many margarines consist of hydrogenated vegetable oils. Read labels and look for margarines that contain liquid vegetable oil as their first ingredient.

FATS AND HYPERTENSION

Hypertension can make hardening of the arteries worse. The lining of blood vessels become thicker to help the walls withstand increased blood pressure. The increased pressure pushes fat deposits into the artery walls. Deposits in the arteries harden into tough, fibrous projections making arteries less elastic and narrow. Narrowed arteries that are less elastic interfere with blood flow to the kidney, heart, and brain.

High blood cholesterol levels may be influenced by several factors.

- **Heredity** may affect the body's ability to regulate cholesterol.

- **High cholesterol diets** may also increase blood levels. Research indicates a high blood cholesterol level combined with other risk factors such as high blood pressure, overweight, smoking, stress, and lack of exercise can lead to heart disease.

- **The kind and the amount of fat in the diet** may influence blood cholesterol levels as well as the development of hardening of the arteries. Fats, especially saturated fats, increase the production of cholesterol in the body.

- **Medications** prescribed to control hypertension may, as a side effect, cause blood levels of cholesterol and triglycerides to increase. It is, therefore, important to keep dietary levels of fats low when you take medicine for high blood pressure.

DIETARY FAT

The U.S. dietary goals recommend decreasing total fat levels to 30 percent of our diet from the present 42 percent. The U.S. dietary goals recommend that saturated fats should only be 10 percent of the total fat we eat instead of the present 16 percent.

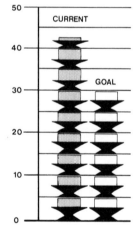

Fat Goal

The average American consumes 600 mg of cholesterol a day but the U.S. dietary goals recommend no more than 300 mg a day. The chart on page 95 lists cholesterol contents of common foods. Can you estimate how much you eat in a day?

SHOPPING FOR HIDDEN FATS

One of the most effective ways of decreasing the fat content of your diet is to shop wisely. Did you know that some brands of microwave popcorn are more than 50 percent fat, most bologna is over 80 percent fat, and cream of mushroom soup is 63 percent fat? To make wise choices when you shop, read labels. Labels list the amount of fat in a serving by grams. There are 9 calories in 1 gram of fat. To determine the percentage of calories that come from fat in any product remember the following:

a) There are 9 calories in 1 gram of fat.

b) Multiply the grams of fat in a serving times 9. The result equals the number of calories from fat in a serving.

c) Divide the fat calories by the total calories in a serving to determine the percentage of fat in each serving.

For example, using the information on the CHILI label below:

1. There are 10 grams of fat in 1 cup of chili.

2. 10 grams of fat X 9 calories = 90 calories from fat in 1 cup.

3. 90 ÷ 200 = 45 percent of the calories in 1 cup of chili come from fat.

Chili Label

Serving Size	1 cup
Calories	200
Fat	10 g
Carbohydrate	5 g
Sodium	980 mg

Many products are labeled 90 percent or 95 percent fat free. Does this mean they contain only 5 percent to 10 percent fat and are a good nutritional choice? This type of label is misleading. Food companies figure the fat content **by weight** not by calories. Water weighs a lot and is often a main ingredient in many products; but, water has no calories. A package of 95 percent fat-free lunchmeat may have 100 calories and 5 grams of fat in a slice. Calculate the percentage of fat in each slice as you did for the chili:

1. There are 5 grams of fat in each slice.

2. Multiply 5 grams of fat by 9 calories = 45 calories from fat in each slice.

3. 45 ÷ 100 = 45 percent of the calories in each slice of lunchmeat come from fat!

The U.S. Dietary Goals, American Heart Association, American Diabetic Association and The American Dietetic Association all recommend that Americans keep daily levels of dietary fat below 30 percent. Thus, whenever possible, buy products that contain 30 percent or less fat. Some foods such as cheese are naturally high in fat and are seldom less than 30 percent fat. However, a cheese that is 50 percent fat is a better choice than a cheese that is 85 percent fat.

CHOLESTEROL CONTENT OF COMMON FOODS
(Recommended-less than 300 mg a day)

Food	Serving Size	Cholesterol (mg)
Milk		
whole	1 cup	34
2%	1 cup	18
1%	1 cup	10
skim	1 cup	4
Yogurt		
whole	1 cup	29
skim	1 cup	4
Cheese-cottage	1 cup	31
cheddar	1 oz.	30
processed, American	1 oz.	27
mozzarella, part-skim	1 oz.	16
Ice Cream		
regular, vanilla	1 cup	59
ice milk, vanilla	1 cup	18
sherbet, orange	1 cup	14
Cream		
heavy	1 Tbsp.	21
half & half	1 Tbsp.	6
sour cream	1 Tbsp.	5
Meat		
liver, fried calf	3-1/2 oz.	438
egg, boiled	1 large	213
shrimp, fried	3-1/2 oz.	120
chicken, w/skin (fried)	3-1/2 oz.	90
haddock, fried	3-1/2 oz.	60
hot dog	1 frank	22

SELECTING LOW-FAT FOODS

Group	Low-Fat Choices	High-Fat Choices
Milk	2%, 1%, skim, low-fat yogurt, ice milk	whole milk, ice cream, cheddar cheese
Meat & Meat Substitutes	fish, chicken, lean beef, lean pork, eggs, beans,	fried meats, fatty meats such as bacon, sausage, lunch meats, spare ribs, hot dogs
Vegetable & Fruit	all fruits & vegetables - cooked plain	french fries, fried & creamed vegetables, coconut, avocado
Bread & Cereal	all breads, pastas, cereals	donuts, waffles pancakes, sweet rolls, biscuits
Salad Dressing & Gravies	natural meat juice gravies, dressings made with low-fat yogurt, low-fat dressings	mayonnaise, salad dressings, cream cheese, sour cream, gravies, & cream sauces
Desserts	angel food cake, fruit gelatin, sherbet, frozen yogurt	commercially baked products, pies, cookies, desserts made with whole milk, yolks & fat
Snacks	plain popcorn, pretzels	potato & corn chips, flavored crackers, most microwave popcorn

HINTS FOR LOWERING FAT AND
CHOLESTEROL IN RECIPES

Ingredients	Substitutes
1 whole egg	1/4 cup egg substitute *or* 1 egg white + 2 tsp. oil *or* 2 egg whites
1 cup butter	1 cup margarine *or* 7/8 cup oil
1 cup hydrogenated shortening or lard	1 cup oil *or* 1 cup + 3 Tbsp. margarine
1 cup whole milk	1 cup skim milk
1 cup buttermilk	1 Tbsp. lemon juice or vinegar plus skim milk to make 1 cup
1 cup light cream or half & half	3 Tbsp. oil & skim milk to = 1 cup *or* 1 cup evaporated skim milk
1 cup heavy cream or whipping cream	2/3 cup skim milk + 1/3 cup oil
1 cup sour cream	1 cup plain yogurt *or* 1 cup low-fat, low-salt cottage cheese puréed in blender
Ground beef	Ground turkey or chicken
1 oz. (1 square) baking chocolate	3 Tbsp. powdered cocoa + 1 Tbsp. oil
1 cup ice cream	1 cup ice milk *or* 1 cup sherbet

FRENCH DRESSING

INGREDIENTS IN HOMEMADE DRESSING

1/2 cup vegetable oil

1/4 cup lemon juice or vinegar

1/2 tsp. dry mustard

Pinch of paprika

1/8 tsp. onion powder

1/8 tsp. garlic powder

PREPARATION

1. Shake thoroughly all ingredients in a small glass jar.
2. Chill before serving. Makes 3/4 cup.

NUTRIENTS IN 1 TBSP.

	Packaged Mix	Homemade
Calories	82	82
Fat	8	9
Carbohydrate	2	trace
Cholesterol	3	0
Potassium	9	7
Calcium	4	1
Sodium	203	1

LIME DRESSING

INGREDIENTS

1/2 cup low-fat mayonnaise

2 Tbsp. lime juice

1 Tbsp. honey

PREPARATION

1. Mix all ingredients thoroughly.

2. Cover and chill. Serve over fresh fruit. Makes about 3/4 cup.

NUTRIENTS IN 1 TBSP.

Calories	19
Fat	1
Carbohydrate	3
Cholesterol	1
Potassium	4
Calcium	2
Sodium	30

MOCK HOLLANDAISE SAUCE

INGREDIENTS

1 Tbsp. cornstarch

1 cup homemade chicken broth (or low-salt chicken bouillon)

4 tsp. lemon juice

2 Tbsp. margarine

1/4 cup shredded low-fat cheddar cheese

PREPARATION

1. Mix cornstarch and a little broth to make a smooth paste.

2. Add remaining broth, lemon juice, and melted margarine. Cook over low heat stirring constantly. Cook just until mixture begins to boil, about 3 mins.

3. Add cheese stirring until melted. Makes about 1-1/4 cup.

NUTRIENTS IN 1 TBSP.

Calories	17
Fat	1
Carbohydrate	trace
Cholesterol	1
Potassium	3
Calcium	11
Sodium	27

PINEAPPLE CHICKEN

INGREDIENTS

4 chicken breast halves

2 Tbsp. vegetable oil

1 green pepper, chopped

1 cup chopped fresh mushrooms

1-1/2 cups pineapple chunks, drained (save juice)

2/3 cup pineapple juice (add chicken broth to make 2/3 cup)

1/4 tsp. ginger

1-1/2 Tbsp. cornstarch

PREPARATION

1. Skin chicken and cut into bite-sized pieces. Cook for 1 minute in oil. Remove chicken.

2. Add vegetables and cook just until tender. Add pineapple and chicken.

3. Blend cornstarch and ginger into broth. Add to chicken and vegetable mixture. Serve over rice. Makes 4 servings.

NUTRIENTS IN 1 BREAST HALF

Calories	275
Fat	10
Carbohydrate	18
Cholesterol	73
Potassium	494
Calcium	36
Sodium	66

BEEF STROGANOFF

INGREDIENTS

1 lb. sirloin steak, trim fat

1 Tbsp. + 2 tsp. margarine

1/4 cup chopped onion

1 cup sliced fresh mushrooms

1/2 tsp. basil

1 cup plain low-fat yogurt

1 Tbsp. cornstarch

PREPARATION

1. Cut beef into thin strips. Cook beef and onions in 1 Tbsp. margarine for 5 minutes. Turn meat to brown evenly.

2. Remove meat and onions from pan. Add 2 tsp. of margarine to pan and sauté mushrooms just until tender.

3. Add beef, onions, and seasonings to pan with mushrooms.

4. Add 1 Tbsp. cornstarch to 1 Tbsp. yogurt. Stir into remaining yogurt. Add yogurt and cornstarch mixture to meat and stir gently. Heat mixture until just hot but do not boil. Serve over hot noodles. Serves 4.

NUTRIENTS IN 1/2 CUP

Calories	311
Fat	13
Carbohydrate	7
Cholesterol	95
Potassium	714
Calcium	119
Sodium	171

STUFFED FLOUNDER

INGREDIENTS

1 tsp. margarine

1/2 cup chopped onion

1 cup fresh mushrooms

1/2 cup chopped celery

4 slices whole wheat bread

2/3 cup homemade chicken broth
(or low-salt chicken bouillon)

1 Tbsp. chopped parsley

1 tsp. poultry seasoning

Pepper to taste

2 Tbsp. lemon juice

1 lb. flounder or other fish fillets

PREPARATION

1. Sauté onion, sliced mushrooms, and celery in margarine until tender.

2. Toast bread and crumble into bowl. Add sautéed vegetables broth, parsley, and seasonings.

3. Place fillets in baking dish coated with cooking spray. Top each with stuffing mixture and roll in jellyroll fashion. Secure with toothpick.

4. Sprinkle with lemon juice and bake, uncovered, for 25 to 30 minutes at 350° until fish flakes with fork. Serves 8.

NUTRIENTS IN 1 FILLET

Calories	221
Fat	8
Carbohydrate	11
Cholesterol	trace
Potassium	580
Calcium	43
Sodium	326

POACHED FISH

INGREDIENTS

1 lb. haddock, flounder or sole   Peppercorns

Whole cloves   1 bay leaf

1 small onion

4 tsp. lemon or 1/4 cup vinegar

PREPARATION

1. Fill skillet 3/4 with water. Add all ingredients and let simmer.

2. Add fish and poach until fish flakes with fork. Serve with lemon juice or low-fat sauce. Serves 4.

NUTRIENTS PER SERVING

Calories	167
Fat	8
Carbohydrate	2
Cholesterol	0
Potassium	437
Calcium	24
Sodium	83

RICE-PORK DINNER

INGREDIENTS

4 pork chops, trimmed of fat

2 tsp. margarine

1 small onion, chopped

1/2 cup chopped green pepper

1/2 cup uncooked rice

14 oz. can crushed no-salt-added tomatoes

1/4 cup water

1/2 tsp. dry mustard

1 tsp. Italian seasoning

1/2 tsp. salt

PREPARATION

1. Brown pork chops on both sides in skillet coated with cooking spray. Remove chops and drain on paper towel.

2. Sauté onion and green pepper in margarine. Stir in rice, tomatoes, water, mustard, seasoning, and pork chops. Cover and simmer 25 to 30 minutes until rice is tender and pork chops are done. Serves 4.

NUTRIENTS PER SERVING

Calories	296
Fat	12
Carbohydrate	24
Cholesterol	63
Potassium	554
Calcium	44
Sodium	329

MEAT LOAF

INGREDIENTS

1-1/2 lb. lean ground beef   1/4 cup diced onion

1 cup no-salt-added tomato juice   Pepper as desired

3/4 cup uncooked oats   1/4 tsp. salt

1 egg, slightly beaten

PREPARATION

1. Combine all ingredients in mixing bowl. Mix thoroughly.

2. Press mixture firmly into an ungreased loaf pan (8x4x2). Bake at 350° about one hour. Let stand 5-10 minutes before serving. Serves 8.

NUTRIENTS IN 1" SLICE

Calories	265
Fat	15
Carbohydrate	7
Cholesterol	105
Potassium	368
Calcium	14
Sodium	131

Frozen commercial meatloaf can contain more than 1300 mg of sodium and 27 g of fat in 8 oz.

BAKED PARMESAN CHICKEN

INGREDIENTS

1/4 to 1/3 cup dry bread crumbs

1 Tbsp. parsley flakes

2 Tbsp. grated parmesan cheese

4 chicken breast halves, skinned (may bone if desired)

4 tsp. margarine

1 Tbsp. lemon juice

PREPARATION

1. Combine bread crumbs, parsley, and cheese in a small bowl.

2. Coat both sides of chicken in crumb mixture.

3. Melt margarine in a baking dish. Add lemon juice. Coat both sides of chicken with margarine and lemon mixture. Bake, uncovered, at 350° for 45 minutes or until done. Serves 4.

NUTRIENTS IN 1 BREAST HALF

Calories	215
Fat	8
Carbohydrate	5
Cholesterol	75
Potassium	246
Calcium	68
Sodium	213

SWISS STEAK

INGREDIENTS

1/4 cup flour

1 lb. beef round steak, trim fat

Pepper as desired

1 Tbsp. vegetable oil

1/3 cup chopped onion

6 oz. can no-salt-added vegetable juice

16 oz. can no-salt-added tomatoes

1/2 cup homemade beef broth (or low-salt beef bouillon)

1-1/2 cups diced carrots

PREPARATION

1. Trim all fat from steak and coat with flour and pepper. Pound meat with edge of plate or wooden mallet to tenderize. Or, use unsalted meat tenderizer before meat is floured.
2. Heat oil in skillet. Brown steak on both sides. Remove steak from skillet.
3. Sauté onion in skillet. Add tomatoes, beef broth, vegetable juice, and meat. Cover and simmer 1-1/2 hour.
4. Add carrot pieces and simmer 1/2 hour more until carrots are tender. Serves 6.

NUTRIENTS IN 1 SERVING

Calories	226
Fat	7
Carbohydrate	13
Cholesterol	161
Potassium	742
Calcium	48
Sodium	252

Swiss steak frozen dinners can contain more than 1,000 mg of sodium!

STIR FRY

INGREDIENTS

1 Tbsp. margarine   1 tsp. sugar
1/3 cup diced onions
1 Tbsp. vegetable oil
3/4 cup lean pork or chicken
1 cup broccoli
1/2 cup fresh mushrooms
6 oz. package frozen snow peas
8 oz. can water chestnuts, drained
1/2 cup sliced carrots
1 cup homemade chicken broth (or low-salt chicken bouillon)
1 Tbsp. soy sauce (or use low-salt soy sauce)

PREPARATION

1. Sauté onions in margarine in a wok or fry pan. Remove from pan. Add oil and heat until pan is hot enough that one vegetable dropped in oil sizzles.
2. Add meat, stirring quickly to brown. Add vegetables.
3. Combine broth, soy sauce, and sugar. Add to meat and vegetables. Cover pan and cook just until vegetables are tender but still crunchy.
4. To thicken stir fry, add 1 Tbsp. cornstarch to 2 Tbsp. of cold chicken broth or cold water. Serve over rice. Makes 5 cups.

NUTRIENTS IN 1 CUP

Calories	151
Fat	7
Carbohydrate	10
Cholesterol	29
Potassium	324
Calcium	32
Sodium	281

TOMATO-MEAT SHELLS

INGREDIENTS

1/2 lb. lean ground beef
1 medium onion, chopped
1/3 cup chopped celery
1/2 tsp. garlic powder
2-14.5 oz. cans no-salt-added tomatoes
1 bay leaf
Pepper to taste
1/2 tsp. salt
3/4 tsp. Italian seasoning
12 jumbo macaroni shells
1-1/2 cups chopped fresh broccoli or 10 oz. frozen package

15 oz. carton part-skim
   ricotta cheese
2 egg whites
2 oz. grated swiss cheese

PREPARATION

1. Brown beef in large skillet. Add onion, celery, and garlic. Cook until tender — about 5 minutes.

2. Drain off fat. Add tomatoes (do not drain), bay leaf, pepper, salt, and Italian seasoning.

3. Cover and simmer for 25 minutes. Uncover and cook 15 more minutes until sauce thickens. Remove bay leaf.

4. While meat sauce cooks, cook shells in boiling water until tender. Drain. Cook broccoli according to package directions. Drain.

5. Combine broccoli and cheese. Beat egg whites until stiff. Fold into cheese mixture. Fill shells.

6. Spoon 1/2 of meat sauce into a 13 x 9 x 2" baking dish lightly coated with cooking oil spray. Arrange shells open side up in a single layer over meat sauce. Pour remaining sauce over shells. Sprinkle shredded cheese on top. Cover, bake at 350° for about 45 minutes. Serves 6.

NUTRIENTS IN 2 SHELLS

Calories	331
Fat	15
Carbohydrate	24
Cholesterol	62
Potassium	676
Calcium	358
Sodium	354

BEEF STEW

INGREDIENTS IN HOMEMADE RECIPE

1 lb. lean beef chuck, cubed   3 carrots, diced

2 onions, diced   3 med. potatoes, diced

1 stalk celery, diced   1 garlic clove

1 bay leaf   Pepper to taste

1 cup beef stock (or use low-salt beef bouillon)

2 tsp. Worcestershire sauce

PREPARATION

1. Put all ingredients in dutch oven. Cook in 350° oven for 2 hours. Before serving remove bay leaf and garlic clove. Serves 6. If desired, thicken gravy with cornstarch.

NUTRIENTS IN 1 CUP

	Canned	Homemade
Calories	220	232
Fat	11	8
Carbohydrate	15	15
Cholesterol	NA*	68
Potassium	613	515
Calcium	29	34
Sodium	980	96

*NA=not available

CARBOHYDRATES

CARBOHYDRATE: A DEFINITION

Plants make carbohydrates from carbon dioxide in the air, water in the soil, and light. The carbohydrates are then stored in the roots, stems, seeds, and leaves of the plant to be used for energy and growth. When people eat any part of those plants, they eat either *complex or simple carbohydrates,* supplying their bodies with a potential source of energy.

Complex carbohydrates, or "starches," are broken down by the body gradually, over a two to four hour period, thus providing a steady supply of energy to the tissues until the next regular meal. The following

are examples of complex carbohydrates: bread, pasta, cereal, and starchy vegetables such as corn, peas, beans, and potatoes.

Simple carbohydrates (sugars) can be broken down by the body in one to ten minutes, quickly supplying energy to the body. The following are examples of simple carbohydrates: naturally occurring sugars which are found in dairy products, vegetables, fruits and fruit juices, and refined sugars such as honey, molasses, and brown, powdered, and white sugar. Ice cream, candy bars, and soda pop are made with refined sugars.

CARBOHYDRATES AND HYPERTENSION

The body breaks down carbohydrates to their simplest form — *glucose* (often called blood sugar). Glucose is used by all the tissues in our body for energy. Medications prescribed to control high blood pressure can cause an undesirable increase in blood glucose levels. To counteract this side effect, <u>simple</u> <u>carbo-</u>

hydrates should be kept low in the diet. Complex carbohydrates should be increased in the diet because they cause a slower rise in blood sugar levels over a longer period of time.

DIETARY CARBOHYDRATES

Unlike our ancestors, Americans today eat fewer complex carbohydrates such as wholegrain breads and cereals, and potatoes and more foods containing refined sugars such as pop and candy. The U.S. dietary goals suggest that 55 to 60 percent of the foods we eat daily should be carbohydrates with an emphasis on complex carbohydrates.

Most of the sugar we eat comes from processed foods such as canned fruits, jams and jellies, cereals, boxed cakes, and bakery products. Sugar can be disguised in many ways on a label. Corn syrup, honey, cane syrup, dextrose, and corn sweeteners are all terms that mean sugar. It pays to read labels.

To reduce simple sugars in your diet:

- **choose foods canned in water** or their own juice.

- **read labels** on cereal boxes. Carbohydrates are listed as starch (or complex), sucrose (or simple), and fiber. Cereals that contain six grams or less of sucrose (sugar) are considered low in simple sugars. The higher the grams of **complex** carbohydrates the better!

CARBOHYDRATE INFORMATION		
	WITH ½ CUP	
	CEREAL	VITAMINS A & D SKIMMILK
STARCH AND RELATED CARBO- HYDRATES	15 g	15 g
SUCROSE & OTHER SUGARS	6 g	12 g
DIETARY FIBER	3 g	3 g
TOTAL CAR- BOHYDRATES		30 g

- **reduce sugar in recipes.** Make your own cookies, muffins, and puddings and reduce the sugar. Cut back slowly in cakes and yeast breads because sugar provides texture and height.

- **when eating out,** complex carbohydrates such as potatoes, breads, and pasta are excellent choices. But, watch what you put on them. Ask for margarine, sour cream, or grated cheese on the side so you can control the amount. Natural, simple carbohydrates such as vegetables and fruits are also good choices but leave off the sauces and don't smother those salads with extra fats and salt.

Salad Base:	Calories
1/4 head lettuce	20
1/2 cucumber	5
1/2 green pepper	8
1 small tomato	25
1 small carrot	30
5 mushrooms	10
Total	**98**
Toppings Added:	
1/2 cup cottage cheese	110
1 oz. cheese, grated	115
2 Tbsp. bacon bits	76
1/3 cup croutons	120
3 Tbsp. Italian dressing	255
Total	**676!**

Recipes in this chapter emphasize complex carbohydrates such as breads, pastas, grains, and potatoes. Also included are traditional cake, cookie, and sauce recipes in which the sugar, fat, and salt content have been reduced. Remember, however, that these foods should be limited in your diet; just because the calories have been reduced doesn't mean you can eat larger portions!

DUMPLINGS

INGREDIENTS

1 cup flour   1 Tbsp. margarine

2 tsp. baking powder   3/4 cup skim or 1% milk

1/2 cup dry Cream of Wheat

PREPARATION

1. Combine flour and baking powder. Stir in Cream of Wheat.

2. Cut in margarine with pastry cutter or two table knives until mixture looks like coarse meal.

3. Add milk and stir to make a soft dough.

4. Drop by teaspoonfuls into hot stew or soup. Cover quickly and steam until done, about 15 minutes. Makes 24 dumplings.

NUTRIENTS IN 2 DUMPLINGS

Calories	58
Fat	1
Carbohydrate	10
Cholesterol	trace
Potassium	38
Calcium	33
Sodium	76

BANANA PANCAKES

INGREDIENTS

1-1/4 cups flour

2 tsp. sugar

2 tsp. baking powder

1 egg

1 cup skim or 1% milk

1 tsp. vegetable oil

1 ripe banana

PREPARATION

1. Mix flour, sugar, and baking powder in small mixing bowl.

2. Beat egg slightly, add milk and oil. Add to dry ingredients.

3. Mash banana and stir in.

4. Pour about 2 Tbsp. batter into a hot nonstick fry pan. Cook on one side until bubbles form then turn. Makes ten, 5" pancakes.

NUTRIENTS IN TWO 5" PANCAKES

Calories	184
Fat	3
Carbohydrate	34
Cholesterol	56
Potassium	220
Calcium	96
Sodium	175

GRANOLA

INGREDIENTS

6 cups oats, regular or quick

1 cup wheat germ

1/2 cup sesame seeds

1/4 cup packed brown sugar

1/3 cup chopped unsalted almonds

1/2 cup unsalted sunflower seeds

1 cup raisins, chopped dates, or apricots

4 Tbsp. vegetable oil

2/3 cup water

1-1/2 tsp. vanilla

1/2 cup honey

PREPARATION

1. Mix dry ingredients in a large bowl.
2. Combine remaining liquid ingredients. Mix well and pour over oats mixture. Stir all ingredients well.
3. Spread mixture into 15 x 10 x 1" jelly-roll pan coated lightly with cooking oil spray. Bake at 350° for 30 minutes until golden brown. Stir every 5 minutes. Cool. Mix in raisins. Makes 10 cups. Store in an air-tight container.

NUTRIENTS IN 1/3 CUP

Calories	170
Fat	7
Carbohydrate	24
Cholesterol	0
Potassium	170
Calcium	36
Sodium	2

OATMEAL AND FRUIT

INGREDIENTS

1 cup skim or 1% milk

1 cup oats, regular or quick

1 apple, peeled & diced

1/4 tsp. cinnamon

1/8 tsp. nutmeg

1 cup plain lowfat yogurt

1 Tbsp. packed brown sugar

PREPARATION

1. In medium saucepan, mix milk, oats, and apple with 1 cup water. Cover and simmer for 5-8 minutes, stirring occasionally, until oatmeal is thickened.

2. Remove from heat and stir in cinnamon and nutmeg.

3. Divide oatmeal evenly into four bowls and top each with 1/4 cup of yogurt and 3/4 tsp. of brown sugar. Makes 4 cups.

NUTRIENTS IN 1 CUP

Calories	172
Fat	3
Carbohydrate	29
Cholesterol	5
Potassium	347
Calcium	185
Sodium	72

Instant packages of oatmeal can contain more than 300 mg of sodium!

APPLE MUFFINS

INGREDIENTS

1-1/2 cups flour

1/3 cup sugar

2 tsp. baking powder

1 tsp. cinnamon

1/2 tsp. nutmeg

1/4 tsp. salt

1 cup chopped apple

1 cup skim or 1% milk

1 egg

2 Tbsp. vegetable oil

PREPARATION

1. Combine flour, sugar, baking powder, cinnamon, nutmeg, salt, and apples in a large mixing bowl.
2. Combine milk, slightly beaten egg, and oil in smaller bowl. Make a well in center of dry ingredients and add liquid ingredients.
3. Stir just until moistened. Batter will still be lumpy.
4. Coat muffin pans with cooking spray and fill 1/2 full with batter. Bake at 400° for 25 minutes. Makes 12 muffins. For blueberry muffins, substitute 1 cup drained fresh or frozen blueberries. Omit the cinnamon and nutmeg.

NUTRIENTS IN 1 MUFFIN

Calories	124
Fat	3
Carbohydrate	22
Cholesterol	23
Potassium	80
Calcium	43
Sodium	113

= BRAN and FRUIT MUFFINS =

INGREDIENTS

1 cup all-purpose flour

2 tsp. baking powder

1/3 cup packed brown sugar

1 cup skim or 1% milk

2-1/2 cups bran flake cereal

1 egg

1/4 cup vegetable oil

1/2 cup chopped dates, apricots or prunes

PREPARATION

1. Combine flour, baking powder, and sugar in large mixing bowl.
2. Pour milk over cereal in another bowl and let stand for about three minutes. Mix slightly.
3. To slightly beaten egg, add oil. Add to milk and cereal mixture. Stir in chopped fruit.
4. Make a well in dry ingredients and add milk and cereal mixture. Stir only until slightly moistened. Batter will still be lumpy.
5. Coat muffin pan with cooking spray. Fill 2/3 with batter. Bake at 400° for 25 minutes until brown. Makes 12 muffins.

NUTRIENTS IN 1 MUFFIN

Calories	162
Fat	5
Carbohydrate	27
Cholesterol	23
Potassium	170
Calcium	50
Sodium	150

LENTIL PUDDING

INGREDIENTS

1 medium onion, diced

1 Tbsp. vegetable oil

1 cup dried lentils

4 cups water

1 bayleaf

1/2 tsp. allspice

1/4 tsp. salt

Pepper to taste

1/4 cup rice

PREPARATION

1. Sauté onion in oil.

2. Rinse lentils and simmer with bayleaf in water for 45 minutes.

3. Add salt, allspice, pepper, onion, and rice to lentils. Cook until rice is done. The mixture will be slightly liquid but will thicken as it cools.

4. Remove bayleaf. Serve with pita bread. Makes 4 cups.

NUTRIENTS IN 1 CUP

Calories	211
Fat	4
Carbohydrate	36
Cholesterol	0
Potassium	358
Calcium	43
Sodium	160

RICE PILAF

INGREDIENTS

1 medium onion, diced

1 tsp. margarine

1 cup long-grain rice

2 cups homemade chicken broth
(or low-salt chicken bouillon)

1 medium tomato, diced

1 Tbsp. parsley

1/2 tsp. salt

PREPARATION

1. Sauté onion in margarine.

2. Cook rice in chicken broth until done.

3. Add parsley, onion, tomato, and salt to rice during last 10 minutes of cooking. Makes 4 cups cooked rice.

NUTRIENTS IN 1/2 CUP

Calories	103
Fat	4
Carbohydrate	23
Cholesterol	0
Potassium	76
Calcium	11
Sodium	143

Instant and flavored rice in a box can contain more than 650 mg of sodium in 1/2 cup!

PEANUT BUTTER COOKIES

INGREDIENTS

1/2 cup margarine	1 tsp. vanilla
1/4 cup sugar	1-1/4 cup flour
1/4 cup brown sugar	1 tsp. baking powder
1 egg	
1/2 cup low-sodium peanut butter	

PREPARATION

1. Cream margarine with sugars.
2. Stir in egg, peanut butter, and vanilla.
3. Combine flour and baking powder. Add to margarine mixture and beat.
4. Make dough into 1" balls and place on cookie sheet coated lightly with cooking spray.
5. Flatten each ball with a fork dipped in flour. Bake at 350° for about 15 minutes. Cool cookies for 2 minutes before removing from sheet. Makes 3 dozen.

NUTRIENTS IN 1 COOKIE

Calories	72
Fat	5
Carbohydrate	7
Cholesterol	8
Potassium	13
Calcium	5
Sodium	43

BANANA CAKE

INGREDIENTS

3-3/4 cups flour

3 tsp. baking powder

1 tsp. baking soda

1 cup margarine, softened

1 cup sugar

2 eggs

1/4 cup plain lowfat yogurt

2 cups ripe bananas

PREPARATION

1. Combine flour, baking powder, and soda into large bowl.

2. Combine margarine, sugar, and eggs in large bowl. Beat until light and fluffy.

3. Stir yogurt into mashed bananas. Alternate adding flour mixture and banana mixture into margarine, beating until smooth.

4. Pour batter into a 12-1/2 x 9 x 2" pan coated with cooking spray. Smooth top with a knife or spatula.

5. Bake at 350° for 50 minutes or until cake springs back. Cool and cut into 24 pieces.

NUTRIENTS IN 1 PIECE

Calories	195
Fat	8
Carbohydrate	28
Cholesterol	23
Potassium	112
Calcium	21
Sodium	173

POUND CAKE

INGREDIENTS

1 cup sugar

1 cup margarine, softened

2 eggs

2-1/4 cup flour

1/2 tsp. baking soda

1 tsp. vanilla

1 tsp. grated lemon rind

8 oz. lowfat peach yogurt

PREPARATION

1. Gradually beat sugar into margarine until mixture is light and fluffy.
2. Add eggs, one at a time, beating after each addition.
3. Combine flour and soda. Add to creamed mixture.
4. Stir lemon rind, vanilla, and yogurt into batter. Pour batter into 10" Bundt pan coated with cooking spray. Bake at 350° for one hour or until toothpick comes out clean. Cool in pan for 15 minutes. Remove from pan and cool on rack. Serve with fresh fruit or low-calorie sauce. Makes 24-1" slice.

NUTRIENTS IN 1" PIECE

Calories	156
Fat	8
Carbohydrate	19
Cholesterol	23
Potassium	39
Calcium	22
Sodium	117

WHITE CAKE

INGREDIENTS IN HOMEMADE RECIPE

2 cups flour
1 Tbsp. baking powder
1 cup sugar
3 egg whites

1/2 cup vegetable oil
3/4 cup skim or 1% milk
1 tsp. vanilla

PREPARATION

1. Combine flour, baking powder, and 3/4 cup sugar.
2. Beat egg whites gradually adding 1/4 cup sugar until stiff peaks form.
3. Combine oil, 1/2 cup milk, and vanilla. Make a well in the dry ingredients and add liquids. Beat 1 minute at medium speed, add remaining milk and beat another minute.
4. Carefully fold egg whites into cake batter.
5. Divide batter into 2, 8" layer cake pans coated with cooking spray. Bake at 375° about 30 minutes until cake springs back. Cool 10 minutes before removing from pans. Cake can be served with fresh fruits as a topping or a low-calorie frosting. Makes about 24 pieces.

NUTRIENTS IN 1 PIECE

	Boxed Mix	Homemade
Calories	250	113
Fat	8	5
Carbohydrate	45	16
Cholesterol	NA*	trace
Potassium	82	29
Calcium	70	19
Sodium	238	53

*NA=not available

BLUEBERRY SAUCE

INGREDIENTS

1 Tbsp. cornstarch

1/4 cup sugar

1/2 tsp. cinnamon

1/2 cup water

2-1/2 cups fresh or frozen blueberries

PREPARATION

1. Combine cornstarch, sugar, cinnamon, and water in small saucepan. Bring to a boil. Boil for 1/2 minute stirring constantly.

2. Add blueberries and return to a boil. Boil gently for 2 minutes. Cool. Serve over cake or ice cream. Other fruit such as raspberries, strawberries, or peaches may be substituted for blueberries. Makes about 2-1/2 cups.

NUTRIENTS IN 1/4 CUP

Calories	42
Fat	trace
Carbohydrate	11
Cholesterol	0
Potassium	33
Calcium	4
Sodium	2

CHOCOLATE SAUCE

INGREDIENTS IN HOMEMADE RECIPE

6 Tbsp. unsweetened cocoa

1/3 cup sugar

1/2 cup skim or 1% milk

1/4 cup water

1/2 tsp. vanilla

PREPARATION

1. Combine cocoa and sugar in small saucepan.

2. Stir in milk and water. Continue stirring until smooth.

3. Bring mixture to a boil, stirring constantly. Boil for 1 minute. Cool and add vanilla. Makes 3/4 cup.

NUTRIENTS IN 2 TBSP.

	Canned	Homemade
Calories	90	68
Fat	1	1
Carbohydrate	24	14
Cholesterol	0	trace
Potassium	106	123
Calcium	6	33
Sodium	20	12

PEACH COBBLER

INGREDIENTS

2 Tbsp. margarine

2/3 cup flour

1/2 cup sugar

1-1/2 tsp. baking powder

1/4 tsp. salt

2/3 cup skim or 1% milk

2 cups fresh peaches or other fruit such as blueberries

PREPARATION

1. Melt margarine in 1-1/2 quart casserole dish.

2. Combine flour, sugar, baking powder, and salt in small mixing bowl. Slowly stir in milk. Pour batter into casserole.

3. Sprinkle peaches evenly on top of batter. Bake at 350° about 50 minutes. Makes 4 cups.

NUTRIENTS IN 1/2 CUP

Calories	134
Fat	3
Carbohydrate	26
Cholesterol	trace
Potassium	129
Calcium	41
Sodium	107

EATING OUT

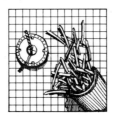

RESTAURANTS

Restaurants and fast food chains offer a special challenge if you are controlling your salt and fat intake. Everyone enjoys eating out occasionally, but it is important to learn how to read menus and identify high-sodium, high-fat foods. It can be done—don't become discouraged! Some helpful hints:

- Ask for dressings "on the side" or carry low-fat salad dressing packets with you.

- Avoid dishes that are prepared with sauces and gravies.

- Request that foods be prepared without salt. This is easier to do when ordering dishes prepared separately, such as vegetables, rather than soups and sauces that are prepared in advance in large quantities.

- Pay attention to processing techniques. A fresh product has less sodium than frozen, frozen less than canned. Don't be afraid to ask if what you're ordering is fresh, frozen, or canned. Or, call ahead and ask!

- Balance a high-sodium dish with a low-sodium dish.

- Margarine has sodium and flavor and will often replace the salt shaker. But, request it "on the side" so you can control the amount!

- Ask for a "doggy bag" when you receive your meal. Cut a suitable portion and bag the rest for a later meal or snack.

- If you're planning a plane trip, call to request a low-sodium meal in advance. When traveling by car, pack low-sodium snacks to balance that irresistable fast-food meal. Take along fresh fruit and vegetables to munch on while driving or to accompany a fast-food hamburger and soft drink.

- When it is necessary to eat out, be sure to plan low-sodium meals for the rest of the day.

FAST FOODS

Most fast foods are high in salt and fat. But, if you remember where the salt is, you can still eat a nutritious meal at a fast-food restaurant. Adding processed cheese and "the works" such as pickle and catsup on a hamburger adds up to a lot of extra sodium. Most fast-food restaurants will leave off the salt on items such as french fries and hamburgers if you ask.

SODIUM IN FAST FOODS *

Cheeseburger	Calories	Sodium (mg)
Cheese	50	234
Meat	95	25
Bun	145	257
Catsup	10	110
Pickle	1	52
Mustard	1	8
Onion	1	0
Grill seasoning	0	40
Total	**303**	**726**

Leave off the cheese (there are calcium sources with less sodium), pickle, catsup, and grill seasoning.

Hamburger		
Meat	95	25
Bun	145	257
Mustard	1	8
Onion	1	0
Total	**242**	**290**

* Values from McDonald's

136

To improve a fast food meal:

- Order low-fat milk or orange juice; skip the high-calorie, high-salt shakes.

- Avoid fried foods to cut down on fat intake. Even chicken, a low-fat meat, is too high in fat when fried. Plain roast beef, broiled, baked, or grilled chicken or fish are best.

- Special order sandwiches without mayonnaise or sauces. Skip the cheese. It is high in sodium and fat. Lettuce, tomato, and mustard are the best additions to a sandwich.

- Order the smallest portion sizes and fill up on salads. The super size hamburger may be on sale but you don't need the extra calories, salt, and fat.

- Don't be fooled by the "visible" salt on foods. Shakes and those quick breakfast items contain much more salt than the fries.

- Order pizzas topped with vegetables such as mushrooms, green peppers, and onions rather than high-fat, high-sodium toppings such as sausage, pepperoni, and extra cheese.

- Salad bars and baked potatoes are excellent choices at fast food restaurants, if you watch what you put on them. Salad dressing and baked potato toppings can contain a lot of sodium, fat, and calories. At the salad bar, pile on the greens and raw vegetables but select low-calorie dressings or use lemon juice. Limit or skip the mayonnaise-based salads, such as potato and macaroni. They are high in calories and fat.

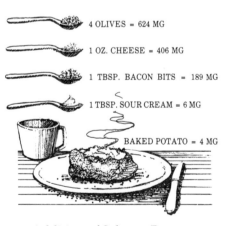

4 OLIVES = 624 MG

1 OZ. CHEESE = 406 MG

1 TBSP. BACON BITS = 189 MG

1 TBSP. SOUR CREAM = 6 MG

BAKED POTATO = 4 MG

Addition of Salt to a Potato

137

FAST FOOD NUTRIENT VALUES

Arby's

Item	Calories	Fat (g)	Sodium (mg)
Light Roast Beef Deluxe	294	10	826
Regular Roast Beef	353	15	936
Light Turkey Deluxe	260	5	1,172
Ham & Cheese	355	14	1,350
Roast Chicken Club	503	27	1,143
Chicken Breast Sandwich	426	22	875
Light Chicken Deluxe	263	6	620
Chicken Fajita Pita	272	9	887
Side Salad	25	0	30
Chef Salad	205	9	692
Potato Cakes	204	12	397
Jamocha Shake	368	11	262

Burger King

Item	Calories	Fat (g)	Sodium (mg)
Hamburger	272	11	505
Cheeseburger	318	15	661
Bacon Double Chzburger	507	30	809
Fish Filet Sandwich	479	33	736
Whopper	614	36	865
Whopper w/cheese	706	44	1,177
Broiler Chicken Sandwich	267	8	728
Chef Salad	178	9	568
Chunky Chicken Salad	142	4	443
Chicken Tenders (6)	236	13	541
Onion Rings	339	19	628
Apple Pie	311	14	412
Chocolate Shake (med.)	326	10	198
Bac'n Brkfst Croissan'wich	353	23	780
French Toast Sticks	538	32	537

McDonald's

Item	Calories	Fat (g)	Sodium (mg)
Hamburger	255	9	490
Cheeseburger	305	13	725
Quarter Pounder	410	20	645
Quarter Pounder w/chz.	510	28	1,110
Big Mac	500	26	890
Filet-O-Fish	370	18	730
McLean Deluxe	320	10	670
Chicken McNuggets (6 pcs)	270	15	580
barbeque sauce	50	0	340
hot mustard	70	4	250
honey	45	0	0
Garden Salad	50	2	70
Chunky Chicken Salad	150	4	230
Croutons	50	2	140
Bacon Bits	15	1	95
Blue Cheese Dressing	250	20	750
Lite Vinaigrette Drsng.	48	2	240
French Fries (small)	220	12	109
Chocolate Lowfat Shake	320	2	240
Vanilla Lowfat Shake	290	1	170
Apple Pie	260	15	240
Chocolate Chip Cookies	330	15	280
Hot Fudge Yogurt Sundae	240	3	170
Vanilla Yogurt Cone	105	1	80
Egg McMuffin	280	11	710
Hot Cakes			
w/margarine & syrup	440	12	685
Scrambled Eggs	140	10	290
Pork Sausage	160	15	310
English Muffin w/spread	170	4	285
Hashbrown Potatoes	130	7	330
Biscuit w/sausage	420	28	1,040
Apple Bran Muffin	180	0	200
Cheerios	80	1	210
Raspberry Danish	410	16	310

Dairy Queen

Item	Calories	Fat (g)	Sodium (mg)
Single Hamburger	310	13	580
Double Hamburger w/chz	570	34	1,070
Hot Dog	280	16	700
Hot Dog w/chili	320	19	720
BBQ Beef Sandwich	225	4	700
Fish Fillet	370	16	630
Chicken Fillet Sandwich	430	20	760
Grilled Chicken Fillet	300	8	800
Chocolate Shake (reg.)	540	14	290
"Dilly" Bar	210	13	50
"Buster Bar"	450	29	220
"Mr. Misty" (reg.)	250	0	0
Cone (small)	140	4	60
Yogurt Cone (reg.)	180	0	80
Yogurt Strawberry Sundae	200	0	80
Heath "Blizzard" (reg.)	680	21	360

Wendy's

Item	Calories	Fat (g)	Sodium (mg)
Hamburger (single)	420	21	890
Hamburger (single w/chz)	490	27	1,150
Big Classic	570	33	1,085
Chicken Sandwich	440	19	725
Plain Potato	270	0	20
Bacon & Cheese Potato	520	18	1,460
Chili (reg.)	220	7	750
French Fries (small)	240	12	145
Frosty (small)	340	10	200
Chicken Nuggets (6)	280	20	600
Grilled Chicken Sandwich	320	9	815
Fish Fillet Sandwich	460	25	780
Chef Salad	130	5	460

Kentucky Fried Chicken

Item	Calories	Fat (g)	Sodium (mg)
Wing, Hot & Spicy	244	18	459
Side Breast, Hot & Spicy	398	27	922
Wing, Original Recipe	172	11	383
Drumstick, Original Recipe	152	9	269
Side Breast, Original Recipe	245	15	604
Wing, Extra Crispy	231	17	319
Drumstick, Extra Crispy	205	14	292
Side Breast, Extra Crispy	379	27	646
Side Breast, Lite 'N Crispy	204	12	417
Drumstick, Lite 'N Crispy	121	7	196
Kentucky Nuggets (6)	284	18	865
Mashed Potatoes & Gravy	71	2	339
Corn-on-the-Cob	90	2	11
Cole Slaw	114	6	177
Buttermilk Biscuit	235	12	655

Taco Bell

Item	Calories	Fat (g)	Sodium (mg)
Bean Burrito	226	9	652
Chicken Burrito	334	12	880
Burrito Supreme	503	22	1,181
Taco	183	11	276
Taco Bellgrande	335	23	472
Chicken MEXIMELT	257	15	779
Taco Salad	905	61	910
Taco Sauce (packet)	2	0	126
Mexican Pizza	575	37	1,031
Tostada	243	11	596
Nachos	346	18	399
Nachos Bellgrande	649	35	997
Cinnamon Twists	171	8	234

Pizza Hut

Item (2 slices medium pizza)	Calories	Fat (g)	Sodium (mg)
Pan Pizza			
Cheese	492	18	940
Pepperoni	540	22	1,127
Supreme	589	30	1,363
Thin 'n Crispy®			
Cheese	398	17	867
Pepperoni	413	20	986
Supreme	459	22	1,328
Hand-Tossed			
Cheese	518	20	1,276
Pepperoni	500	23	1,267
Supreme	540	26	1,470
Personal Pan Pizza® (Whole Pizza)			
Pepperoni	675	29	1,335
Supreme	647	28	1,313

Best Fast Food Meals

A good rule of thumb is to limit meals to no more than 30 percent fat, 100 mg cholesterol, and 1,000 mg sodium. Nutrition information available at most fast food restaurants can be used to combine foods you like into a meal that follows the above guidelines. It is difficult to combine fast foods into a healthy meal. For example, a low-calorie salad comes with a high-sodium salad dressing. Sodium, however, could be controlled by taking your own low-sodium salad dressing, using lemon as a dressing, or consuming only a portion of the packet provided. Diet soda, coffee, or tea can be substituted for higher fat and calorie drinks in any meal. Remember, when you do choose to eat a fast food meal, low-fat, low-sodium, and low-cholesterol foods should be selected the rest of the day.

	Calories	Fat (g)	Sodium (mg)	Cholesterol (mg)
Arby's				
Light Roast Chicken Deluxe	263	6	620	39
Side Salad with	25	0	30	0
1 oz. Weight Watcher's Creamy French	48	3	170	0
Milk (2%)	121	5	122	8

Total Meal = 457 calories, 14 g fat (28%), 942 mg sodium, 47 mg cholesterol

	Calories	Fat (g)	Sodium (mg)	Cholesterol (mg)
Burger King				
Broiler Chicken Sandwich with lettuce, tomato, no sauce	230	4	654	40
Milk (2%)	121	5	122	8

Total Meal = 351 calories, 9 g fat (23%), 776 mg sodium, 48 mg cholesterol

	Calories	Fat (g)	Sodium (mg)	Cholesterol (mg)
Chunky Chicken Salad with	142	4	443	49
1/2 pkg. Light Italian	85	9	381	0
Small Cola (16 oz)	200	0	20	0

Total Meal = 427 calories, 13 g fat (27%), 844 mg sodium, 9 mg cholesterol

	Calories	Fat (g)	Sodium (mg)	Cholesterol (mg)
McDonald's				
Grilled Chicken Sandwich	348	11	421	NA*
Side Salad with	30	1	33	35
1/2 pkg. Lite Red French	80	4	230	0
Milk (1%)	110	2	130	10

Total Meal = 568 calories, 18 g fat (29%) 814 mg sodium, 45+ mg cholesterol
*NA = not available

	Calories	Fat (g)	Sodium (mg)	Cholesterol (mg)
McLean Sandwich	320	10	670	60
Side Salad with	30	1	33	35
1/2 pkg. Lite Vinaigrette	24	1	120	0
Orange Drink (12 oz.)	130	0	10	0
Vanilla Frozen Yogurt Cone	105	1	80	3

Total Meal = 609 calories, 13 g fat (19%), 913 mg sodium, 98 mg cholesterol

	Calories	Fat (g)	Sodium (mg)	Cholesterol (mg)
Chunky Chicken Salad with	150	4	230	78
1/2 pkg. Lite Vinaigrette	24	1	120	0
Orange or Grapefruit Juice	80	0	5	0
Hot Fudge Frozen Yogurt Sundae	240	3	170	6

Total Meal = 494 calories, 8 g fat (15%), 525 mg sodium, 84 mg cholesterol

	Calories	Fat (g)	Sodium (mg)	Cholesterol (mg)
Hamburger without pickle & ketchup	244	9	328	37
Side salad with	30	1	33	35
1/2 pkg. Lite Vinaigrette	24	1	120	0
Vanilla Milk Shake	290	1	170	10

Total Meal = 588 calories, 12 g fat (18%), 651 mg sodium, 82 mg cholesterol.

	Calories	Fat (g)	Sodium (mg)	Cholesterol (mg)
Blueberry Muffin	170	0	220	0
Cheerios	80	1	210	0
Milk (1%)	110	2	130	10
Orange Juice	80	0	0	0

Total Meal = 440 calories, 3 g fat (6%), 560 mg sodium, 10 mg cholesterol

	Calories	Fat (g)	Sodium (mg)	Cholesterol (mg)
Dairy Queen				
BBQ Sandwich	225	4	700	20
Small Cola (12 oz.)	150	0	15	0
DQ Sandwich	140	4	135	5

Total Meal = 515 calories, 8 g fat (14%), 850 mg sodium, 25 mg cholesterol

	Calories	Fat (g)	Sodium (mg)	Cholesterol (mg)
Grilled Chicken Sandwich	300	8	800	50
Diet Cola (12 oz.)	1	0	30	0
Regular Yogurt Cone	180	0	80	5

Total Meal = 481 calories, 8 g fat (15%), 910 mg sodium, 55 mg cholesterol

	Calories	Fat (g)	Sodium (mg)	Cholesterol (mg)
Wendy's				
Chili (regular)	220	7	750	45
Frosty (small)	340	10	200	40

Total Meal = 560 calories, 17 g fat (27%), 950 mg sodium, 85 mg cholesterol

	Calories	Fat (g)	Sodium (mg)	Cholesterol (mg)
Baked Potato with Cheese	420	15	310	10
Lemonade (8 oz.)	90	0	0	0

Total Meal = 510 calories, 15 g fat (26%), 310 mg sodium, 10 mg cholesterol.

	Calories	Fat (g)	Sodium (mg)	Cholesterol (mg)
Grilled Chicken Sandwich with lettuce, tomato, no sauce	270	6	645	55
Frosty (small)	340	10	200	40

Total Meal = 610 calories, 16 g fat (24%), 845 mg sodium, 95 mg cholesterol.

	Calories	Fat (g)	Sodium (mg)	Cholesterol (mg)
KFC				
Lite "N Crispy Center Breast	220	12	416	57
Mashed Potatoes & Gravy	71	2	339	1
Corn-On-The-Cob	90	2	11	1
Small Cola (15 oz.)	188	0	19	0

Total Meal = 569 calories, 16 g fat (25%), 785 mg sodium, 59 mg cholesterol

	Calories	Fat (g)	Sodium (mg)	Cholesterol (mg)
Pizza Hut				
2 slices Thin & Crispy Cheese	398	17	867	NA*
Small Cola (16 oz.)	200	0	20	0

Total Meal = 598 calories, 17 g fat (26%), 887 mg sodium, *cholesterol information not available

MICROWAVE COOKING

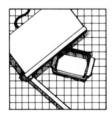

Microwaving

Over 75 percent of the households in the U.S. have a microwave. To keep pace with this growing number of microwaves, food companies are introducing microwave products at a phenomenal rate. Even though these products are convenient, they are often high in sodium and fat.

The most obvious advantage to owning a microwave is its time-saving qualities. Most foods can be prepared in a fraction of the time normally needed. Foods can be reheated very quickly in a serving bowl; there are fewer messy pots to clean up. Foods can also be partially prepared in a microwave and then finished in the conventional way. For example, vegetables for a soup can be partially cooked in a microwave or water can be quickly boiled for gelatin.

In addition to its time-saving benefits, microwave cooking offers the person on a special diet real health benefits. Microwave cooking is good for your health because:

- **Vegetables retain their color, flavor, and nutrients.** Vegetables naturally contain a lot of water. Because liquids don't evaporate during microwaving as they do during conventional top of the stove cooking, vegetables can be cooked in a tightly covered container in very little water. (Only one or two tablespoons of water is usually needed; starchy vegetables, such as potatoes and squash, will need a bit more water.) In addition, because little liquid is needed to microwave, important nutrients are retained and flavor is good even without added salt.

- **Microwaving extracts more fat from meats than the conventional way of cooking.** Anytime fat can be removed there is a health benefit because fat has more than twice the calories of equal portions of protein and carbohydrate. An additional benefit: you don't need to grease pans to prevent sticking.

- **You can braise, stew, steam, poach, stir-fry, and sauté in a microwave oven but you can't deep-fat fry.**

Many people use a microwave for the majority of the cooking they do. However, if you have limited experience cooking with a microwave, there are a few basic facts about microwaving to help ensure success:

- **Shape.** Evenly shaped foods, such as meatloaf, cook differently from irregularly shaped foods like chicken legs. For irregular items, place the thick parts towards the outside edge and the thin parts towards the center of the oven.

- **Density.** Compact foods take longer to cook than porous items. Thus, a baked potato will take longer to cook than a soup. Many foods will need to be rotated 1/4 to 1/2 turn as they cook so they will heat evenly. Rich heavy batters microwave best. Thus, bar cookies microwave better than cakes. Cakes rise higher in a microwave so use less batter.

- **Quantity.** One potato takes much less time to microwave than four. In addition, as the size of the dish increases so does the time. A family-sized casserole will take much longer to cook than several individual ones.

- **Moisture.** Foods high in moisture content such as vegetables microwave very well. Fish and poultry are naturally high in moisture and thus microwave well. Prick thick skins on foods such as potatoes to let steam escape. If steam builds up, foods will burst. Never microwave whole eggs! Pastas and rice take the same amount of water and time as when they are cooked the conventional way. Meats that need a long and slow cooking method to be tender, such as a roast, don't microwave well.

- **Temperature.** A food that is cold will take longer to cook in a microwave than one at room temperature.

- **Utensils.** Glass or microwavable plastic containers should be used for cooking. Paper, glass, or plastic may be used for heating and/or defrosting. Metals should not be used in a microwave oven because they cause the waves to bounce off the dish.

- **Cover food** loosely with paper towels or waxed paper to prevent splattering. Cover food tightly to trap heat and create steam to speed up cooking.

- **Allow standing time** because cooking continues after foods are microwaved. It is wise to underestimate cooking time rather than overestimate. This is why microwave cookbooks give a range of time. Cook your food with the shortest time given, then check to see if it needs the additional time.

- **Browning** doesn't occur in a microwave; thus breads won't brown. Use recipes with dark ingredients like brown sugar, whole wheat flour, or toppings.

There are many good microwave recipe books on the market. Several health-related microwave books are listed in the resource guide at the back of this book. Microwave recipes in this chapter are compared, whenever possible, to similar commercially-prepared products. Remember, most products sold in your grocery store for microwaving are very high in sodium and fat content. Be sure to read labels and shop wisely. Or, **make it yourself in the microwave.** Some general rules to remember when shopping for convenience foods are:

The amount of sodium in a dinner should not be more than 700 mg.

Sodium in a food that will be part of a meal should be 400 mg or less.

A dinner should not be more than 30 percent fat.

POTATO SOUP

INGREDIENTS IN HOMEMADE SOUP

2-1/2 cups cubed potatoes

1 stalk celery, diced

1/3 cup chopped onion

1/4 cup water

1/2 tsp. salt

1 tsp. parsley flakes

1/4 tsp. pepper

2 cups skim or 1% milk

4 Tbsp. flour

3 Tbsp. diet margarine

PREPARATION

1. In a 2 qt. casserole, combine potatoes, celery, onion, water, and seasonings. Cover.

2. Microwave at HIGH until vegetables are tender, about 8 to 10 minutes. Stir halfway through the cooking time.

3. Stir 1/4 cup milk with the flour until smooth.

4. Slowly stir the flour mixture into the remaining milk, margarine, and potato mixture.

5. Microwave at HIGH, uncovered, for 8 to 10 minutes until thick. Stir every 2 to 3 minutes. Makes 4 cups.

NUTRIENTS IN 1 CUP

	Frozen	Homemade
Calories	217	213
Fat	15	5
Carbohydrate	17	36
Cholesterol	NA	2
Potassium	NA	636
Calcium	NA	171
Sodium	791	420

*NA = not available

154

STIR-FRY VEGETABLES

INGREDIENTS IN HOMEMADE RECIPE

2 tsp. olive oil

1/2 cup chopped onions

2 cups thinly sliced cabbage

2 whole carrots, sliced diagonally

1 cup broccoli flowerets

1 cup cauliflower flowerets

2 stalks celery, sliced diagonally

1/2 cup sliced fresh mushrooms

1 tsp. lemon peel

PREPARATION

1. In a 3-qt. casserole place oil and onions. Microwave uncovered at HIGH for 4 minutes.

2. Add remaining vegetables and lemon peel. Stir to mix well. Microwave covered on HIGH for 4 minutes. Makes 4 cups.

   Frozen stir fry vegetables may also be used if no salt has been added.

NUTRIENTS IN 1/2 CUP

	Frozen Commercial	Homemade
Calories	30	34
Fat	0	1
Carbohydrate	7	5
Cholesterol	NA	0
Potassium	NA	242
Calcium	24	28
Sodium	510	23

*NA = not available

CABBAGE ROLLS

INGREDIENTS

8 whole fresh cabbage leaves
1/2 cup water
2-8 oz. cans no-salt-added
   tomato sauce
2 Tbsp. brown sugar
1/2 tsp. salt

2 Tbsp. lemon juice
1 lb. lean ground beef
1/8 tsp. pepper
3/4 cup instant rice
3 Tbsp. chopped onion

PREPARATION

1. In a 3 qt. casserole, place the cabbage leaves and water. Cover with plastic wrap. Microwave until leaves are tender, about 7 to 9 minutes.

2. Stir the tomato sauce, brown sugar, salt, and lemon juice together in a small bowl.

3. Combine the ground beef, pepper, rice, onion, and 3/4 cup of the tomato sauce mixture in a small bowl. Divide the mixture into 8 portions. Place a portion on each of the 8 cabbage leaves. Roll leaf around the meat mixture. Place seam down in casserole dish.

4. Pour remaining sauce over cabbage rolls. Cover with plastic wrap. Microwave at HIGH 13 to 16 minutes. Rotate dish 1/2 turn halfway through cooking time. Let rolls stand for 5 minutes before serving. Makes 8 cabbage rolls.

NUTRIENTS IN 1 ROLL

Calories	249
Fat	9
Carbohydrate	23
Cholesterol	47
Potassium	248
Calcium	24
Sodium	182

STUFFED GREEN PEPPERS

INGREDIENTS

6 small green peppers

1 lb. lean ground beef

2 Tbsp. chopped onion

1/3 cup oats, regular or
    quick

1/2 tsp. salt

1/8 tsp. pepper

1 egg, beaten

1 cup no-salt-added
    spaghetti sauce

PREPARATION

1. Cut off top of green pepper. Remove seeds and membrane.

2. Combine the ground beef, onion, oats, seasonings, egg, and
    1/3 cup spaghetti sauce in a small bowl. Stuff peppers with
    the meat mixture.

3. Place peppers in a 3-qt. casserole. Spread remainder of sauce
    over peppers. Cover with plastic wrap.

4. Microwave 15 to 18 minutes. Turn halfway through cooking
    time. Let stand 5 minutes before serving. Makes 6 peppers.

NUTRIENTS IN 1 PEPPER

Calories	251
Fat	14
Carbohydrate	8
Cholesterol	109
Potassium	413
Calcium	19
Sodium	231

CHICKEN À LA KING

INGREDIENTS IN HOMEMADE RECIPE

3 boneless, skinless chicken breast halves
1/2 cup diced celery
1/3 cup chopped green pepper
1/2 cup sliced fresh mushrooms

1 can, 1/3 less sodium, cream of chicken soup
2 Tbsp. pimento
1 tsp. Worcestershire sauce
1/2 cup skim milk

PREPARATION

1. Cube chicken and microwave until done-about 5 minutes. Drain.

2. Microwave celery, green pepper, and mushrooms at HIGH for 2 minutes. Stir once. Drain.

3. Add soup, pimento, Worcestershire sauce, and milk. Microwave on HIGH for 2 minutes.

4. Stir in cooked chicken. Microwave at HIGH for 5 minutes. Rotate 1/4 turn after 2-1/2 minutes. Serve over rice or toast. Makes 3 cups.

NUTRIENTS IN 1 CUP SERVING

	Frozen Commercial	Homemade
Calories	382	204
Fat	18	6
Carbohydrate	37	8
Cholesterol	NA	78
Potassium	NA	414
Calcium	NA	82
Sodium	554	296

*NA = not available

SUKIYAKI

INGREDIENTS

1/2 lb. sirloin steak

1/4 cup light soy sauce

3 Tbsp. water

2 Tbsp. sugar

1 Tbsp. vegetable oil

1 stalk celery, sliced thin

1/3 cup green onion pieces

1/2 cup fresh bamboo shoots

1/4 cup sliced water chestnuts

1 cup fresh bean sprouts

1 cup sliced fresh mushrooms

PREPARATION

1. Cut sirloin into thin strips, across grain. Strips should be about 1" long.

2. In a small bowl, combine soy sauce, water, and sugar. Set aside.

3. Preheat a large microwaveable dish 5 minutes on HIGH. Add oil. Quickly stir in meat until sizzling stops.

4. Pour soy mixture over meat. Stir in celery, onion, and bamboo shoots.

5. Microwave on HIGH 4 to 6 minutes until vegetables are tender but still crisp. Stir once halfway through cooking.

6. Add remaining vegetables. Microwave 4 to 5 minutes more until mushrooms are tender. Stir once. Makes 4 cups.

NUTRIENTS IN 1/2 CUP

Calories	106
Fat	5
Carbohydrate	6
Cholesterol	25
Potassium	253
Calcium	11
Sodium	280

=FISH IN TOMATO SAUCE=

INGREDIENTS

1 Tbsp. diet margarine

2 cups sliced fresh
mushrooms

1/3 cup chopped onions

1 clove garlic, minced

1-15 oz. can whole no-salt-
added tomatoes

1 tsp. lemon juice

1/2 tsp. salt

1/8 tsp. pepper

1 lb. fish fillets

1 tsp. parsley flakes

PREPARATION

1. Put margarine, mushrooms, onion, and garlic in 12 x 8"
   baking dish. Microwave on HIGH 4 to 6 minutes until
   vegetables are tender. Stir halfway through cooking time.

2. Stir in tomatoes, juice, salt, and pepper.

3. Place fillets in dish with thickest parts turned toward
   outside. Spoon sauce over fillet. Sprinkle with parsley.

4. Microwave on HIGH 5 to 8 minutes until fish flakes easily
   with fork. Rotate dish once halfway through cooking time.
   Serves 4.

NUTRIENTS IN 1 SERVING

Calories	144
Fat	3
Carbohydrate	8
Cholesterol	63
Potassium	733
Calcium	74
Sodium	367

PINEAPPLE UPSIDE DOWN CAKE

INGREDIENTS

1/4 cup diet margarine

1/3 cup packed brown sugar

1-8.25 oz. can pineapple slices, packed in own juice

4 maraschino cherries

1-1/4 cups flour

1/2 cup sugar

2 tsp. baking powder

1/4 cup regular margarine

1 egg

1 tsp. vanilla

PREPARATION

1. Put 1/4 cup diet margarine in a 8" round microwaveable dish. Microwave on HIGH until margarine melts, about 1 minute. Sprinkle sugar over margarine. Drain pineapple (save liquid) and arrange in dish. Decorate center of pineapple rings with cherries, cut in half.

2. In a small bowl, mix flour, sugar, baking powder, regular margarine, egg, pineapple liquid (add water to make 1/2 cup), and vanilla for 3 minutes. Carefully spread batter over pineapple. Microwave on MED HIGH for 12 to 13 minutes. Rotate 1/2 turn halfway through cooking time. Toothpick stuck in cake will come out clean when cake is done.

3. Turn cake upside down onto plate. Let pan stand over cake a few minutes. Serve warm with lemon sauce. Serves 8.

NUTRIENTS IN 1 SERVING

Calories	252
Fat	9
Carbohydrate	40
Cholesterol	34
Potassium	93
Calcium	35
Sodium	228

161

LEMON SAUCE

INGREDIENTS

1/2 cup sugar

1-1/2 Tbsp. cornstarch

1/2 cup water

1/4 cup diet margarine

1/3 cup lemon juice

PREPARATION

1. Combine all ingredients in a 4-cup glass bowl or measuring cup. Microwave on HIGH for 5 to 6 minutes until mixture boils and thickens. Stir once halfway through cooking time. Makes 1-1/4 cup.

NUTRIENTS IN 1 TBSP.

Calories	31
Fat	1
Carbohydrate	6
Cholesterol	0
Potassium	26
Calcium	0
Sodium	5

CARAMEL POPCORN

INGREDIENTS

6 cups popped popcorn

1/2 cup packed brown sugar

3 Tbsp. margarine

1/4 cup light corn syrup

1/2 Tbsp. water

1 tsp. baking soda

PREPARATION

1. In a 3-qt. dish combine the brown sugar, margarine, corn syrup, and water. Microwave at HIGH for 13 to 14 minutes. Stir once at 7 minutes.

2. Quickly add the baking soda to the brown sugar mixture and pour over popcorn.

3. Spread on foil to cool. You may also want to form popcorn balls.

NUTRIENTS IN 1 CUP

Calories	158
Fat	3
Carbohydrate	33
Cholesterol	0
Potassium	64
Calcium	23
Sodium	217

PEANUT BUTTER OATMEAL BARS

INGREDIENTS

4 Tbsp. peanut butter, divided

1/4 cup sugar

1/4 cup brown sugar

2 Tbsp. margarine

1 egg

1/2 tsp. vanilla

1/2 cup flour

1/2 cup quick-cooking rolled oats

1/4 tsp. baking soda

1/2 cup semi-sweet chocolate chips

PREPARATION

1. In a medium bowl, cream 4 Tbsp. peanut butter with sugar, brown sugar, margarine, egg, and vanilla. Beat till fluffy.
2. Stir dry ingredients together in another bowl. Add to creamed mixture and beat.
3. Spread batter in a 8 x 8" baking dish.
4. To prevent overcooking, cover corners with foil triangles.
5. Microwave at HIGH 3 to 5 minutes or until top is no longer wet. Rotate dish 1/4 turn twice during cooking. Cool.
6. Frost bars with melted chocolate chips. Makes 16 bars.

NUTRIENTS IN 1 BAR

Calories	116
Fat	6
Carbohydrate	15
Cholesterol	17
Potassium	74
Calcium	10
Sodium	54

WEIGHT CONTROL

WEIGHT AND HYPERTENSION

There is no doubt that weight loss, if needed, will lower blood pressure. In fact, losing only a few pounds if you are overweight will often lower blood pressure even if an ideal body weight isn't achieved. On the other hand, hypertension may worsen with weight gain.

A quick way to calculate your ideal body weight if you are a female, is to allow 100 pounds for the first 5 feet of height. Add 5 pounds for each additional inch of height. A male should allow 106 pounds for the first 5 feet of height and 6 pounds for each additional inch over 5 feet. For both males and females, add 10% for a large frame and subtract 10% for a small frame. For example, a woman who is 5' 4" tall should ideally weigh about 120 pounds. If she has a large frame her ideal weight would be about 132 pounds.

DIETARY PLAN

An effective weight control program combines a sound dietary plan, exercise and changes in eating habits. A dietary plan should be individualized for each person to be successful. Your physician or local hospital can help you locate a dietitian to develop a well balanced food plan for you.

A three-fourth to one pound loss weekly should be the maximum amount lost. Losing more than this may include water loss and lean body tissue instead of fat, resulting in decreased strength and endurance. Daily caloric intakes of less than 1,200 calories may be low in important nutrients and should be closely supervised by a physician.

Decreasing the amount of fat in your diet is critical for weight loss because fat provides more than twice the calories of carbohydrates and protein. A good food plan should consist of 50 to 55 percent carbohydrate, 15 to 20 percent protein, and 30 percent or less fat. Refer to the chapter on fat for tips on lowering fat in recipes, selecting low-fat foods, and label reading.

EXERCISE AND WEIGHT MAINTENANCE

Basal metabolism is the basic number of calories it takes to maintain involuntary body processes such as breathing. In very low-calorie diets, basal metabolism needs decrease; this means that fewer calories are burned while the body is at rest. Exercise, on the other hand, increases one's basal metabolism. Thus, a combination of **decreased** dietary calories and **increased** exercise is the most effective way to lose weight. Exercise makes weight loss easier and it helps to keep weight off. It increases your ability to concentrate, enables you to sleep better, takes your mind off food, and increases alertness. Refer to the chapter on exercise for more information.

CHANGING DIETARY HABITS

It may not be what you eat so much as when, where, and why you eat. What you do that triggers eating can be extremely important in weight control. How often do you:

- gobble a meal while reading the newspaper or watching TV?
- munch on food while reading, playing cards with friends, or watching TV?
- stop for a snack on the way home from work, everyday?
- eat breakfast on the run, grabbing "empty" calorie foods because you're late to school or work?

It may be necessary to restructure your thoughts and habits on when and why you eat. The first step is to write down for two or three days everything you eat or drink, including the time of the day and what you were doing. It is then possible to rethink why you eat and avoid situations that trigger overeating. For example, take a favorite low-calorie snack to eat on the way home from work, or take an alternate route that bypasses the snack source. Plan and buy one snack for the favorite TV show to prevent a TV binge. If there are no snacks in the house, chances are you won't go out again and get more! Plan a quick but low-calorie, nutritious breakfast the night before school or work such as orange juice, crackers and cheese; eat it while you shave, dress, or put on makeup.

TIPS ON REDUCING YOUR FOOD INTAKE

1. **Go slowly!** Don't try too many changes at once or you'll be overwhelmed and become discouraged. Losing weight takes time.

2. **Set realistic goals.** Make small changes such as substituting a bagel for a danish, a small cola for a large. Small changes add up to large ones.

3. **Include everyday foods** in your diet. Foods you normally eat and that are familiar to you make for a lasting diet. A diet requiring you to eat tuna everyday if you dislike fish is not going to help you permanently change your eating habits.

4. **Eat regular meals.** Skipping meals encourages bingeing later. Dividing your calories into three smaller meals plus small snacks may even be better for you. You don't need to be hungry to lose weight. But, eating all the time can result in weight gain.

5. **Know portion sizes.** Measure your liquids for a few days until you can pour a cup or half cup. A small set of scales will accurately measure three ounces of meat; a ruler helps, too. You may be surprised at just what a "portion" or a "serving" means!

6. **Take time when you eat.** Don't do other activities while you eat. Put your fork down between each bite and chew, chew, chew! When you eat slowly, it allows your stomach time to signal when it's full. Enjoy your food!

7. **Take a walk.** When depressed or anxious, take a walk, treat yourself to a nonedible present, or call someone for support. If you have an urge to eat, wait for ten minutes. You'll usually find something else to do by then and the "urge" will be gone.

8. **Take a list.** When grocery shopping, take a list and shop after you've eaten. Plan your snacks so that large amounts aren't left in your cabinets or refrigerator just waiting to be eaten.

9. **Watch beverages.** Liquids are often forgotten about as sources of calories, but many – including pop and alcohol – are high in calories and these calories add up fast.

10. **DON'T GIVE UP!** If you binge one day or find yourself gorging a hot fudge sundae, don't give up and say you'll always be fat. Say you'll start again.

11. **GIVE YOURSELF A PAT ON THE BACK WHEN YOU SUCCEED!**

WEIGHT CONTROL AND SNACKING

No connection has been shown between the number of times a person snacks during a day and being overweight. Weight gain results when too many calories are consumed in a day and not enough exercise is done.

A light snack can take the hunger pangs out of a weight loss program. If you find yourself snacking too often, try drinking a large glass of ice water, hot tea, or other calorie-free beverage. Brushing your teeth or chewing gum often helps delay the munchies. Or, try another activity you enjoy such as taking a 15 to 20 minute walk, working in the garden, or reading a book.

When you get the munchies, think about the kind of food you are grabbing. Snacks such as potato chips, pretzels, popcorn, nuts, crackers, and corn chips can be high in salt. These snacks are all available in low-salt versions. Snacks can also contain large amounts of fat. Potato chips, buttered popcorn, nuts, and some types of snack crackers are often more than 50 percent fat. The easiest way to select snacks is to use the food groups as a guide. Refer to the Good Snack Guide below for healthy, low-fat snacks in each of the food groups.

GOOD SNACK GUIDE	
Dairy Group	Low-fat shakes, low-fat cheese cubes, yogurt, yogurt shakes, frozen yogurt, hot chocolate made with low-fat milk, puddings made with low-fat milk.
Fruit & Vegetable Group	Frozen fruit juice popsicles, fresh vegetables served with a low-fat dip, fresh fruit wedges, fruit shakes made with fresh fruit & frozen yogurt, fruit juice mixed with diet soda or soda water.
Meat Group	Peanut butter on rice cakes, hard-cooked egg, low-fat cheese wedges, low-fat lunchmeats.
Bread Group	Bagels, quick breads, muffins, tortillas spread with grated cheese & broiled, pita bread spread with cheese & broiled, plain popcorn, English muffin, unsweetened cereal, animal crackers, vanilla wafers, pretzels, graham crackers, bread sticks.

On occasion, everyone gets hungry for a sweet snack. To keep these episodes under control, select lower calorie dessert snacks in small amounts. And, keep sweet snacks out of the house to keep temptation away. Refer to the Under 150 Calorie Goodie List for occasional sweet snack ideas.

UNDER 150 CALORIE GOODIE LIST

Food	Calories
14 pieces or 1 oz. Bridge Mix	140
1 oz. piece of chocolate fudge	122
1 oz. chocolate coated peanuts	150
1 oz. chocolate coated raisins	120
4 Kraft caramels or chocolate fudgies	140
15 Kraft party or butter mints	120
6 chocolate Kisses	148
1 oz. Junior Mints	120
10 Lifesavers	90
4 large marshmallows	100
1 regular brownie from most mixes	130-150
2″ square gingerbread from most mixes	100
1 Hostess crumb cake	130
1 Hostess HoHo	120
1 Hostess Lil'angels	90
2 Almost Home apple, blueberry or cherry fruit sticks	140
2 Almost Home chocolate chip cookies	130
2 homemade chocolate chip cookies	92
2 homemade oatmeal cookies	124
2 chocolate coated graham crackers	124
3 Oreos	140
1 cake doughnut	105
1 fruit juice bar	35-80
1 pudding pop	about 75
1 Weight Watcher's double fudge bar	60
1 Weight Watcher's chocolate treat	100
2 Tbsp. Kraft chocolate topping	100

EXERCISE

EXERCISE & HYPERTENSION

There is no doubt that regular exercise can lower blood pressure in many people with hypertension. Studies have shown significant differences in blood pressure between people who exercise regularly and those who don't. Some studies have even shown regular exercise may prevent hypertension. The best news is that for most people moderate exercise is just as effective as intense exercise in controlling high blood pressure.

Exercise may lower blood pressure more in some people than in others. Women, people who have lower bodyweights, those with a higher diastolic blood pressure, and people who make a long term commitment to exercise seem to benefit the most.

Studies have shown that following aerobic exercise of 30 to 45 minutes, blood pressure remains lower for 1 to 3 hours. Once blood pressure is lowered, regular exercise (approximately three times per week) may maintain the lower levels.

Exercise can also help with weight loss (see the Weight Control chapter). Fifteen minutes of a moderate exercise, such as walking one mile, will burn up 100 extra calories a day. The energy used up from activities is greater for heavier people because they have more weight to move. A person weighing 150 pounds would use more calories walking one mile than a 120 pound person who walks the same distance. Refer to the chart on page 176 for caloric expenditures for activities in your weight category.

Exercise offers other benefits in addition to a decrease in blood pressure and weight loss. An increase in exercise can also reduce stress and anxiety and raise levels of the good type of cholesterol, HDL.

It is important to realize, however, that exercise is not a cure-all. It doesn't result in normalization of blood pressure for all people. It may still be necessary to combine exercise with drug therapy and a good diet in order to keep your blood pressure normal.

Walking at 2 miles an hour	=	about 1 calorie per pound per hour.
Walking at 3.5 miles an hour	=	about 2 calories per pound per hour.
Bicycling slow	=	1.2 calories per pound per hour
Bicycling fast	=	2.6 calories per pound per hour
Running at 5 miles an hour	=	3.5 calories per pound per hour
Swimming at 1 mile an hour	=	3 calories per pound per hour

Now that you know the value of exercise in controlling hypertension, the next step is to plan your exercise program. Before you begin an exercise program:

1) See a doctor. It is important to have a medical evaluation before beginning any exercise program.

2) Stop if you experience pain. It isn't necessary to sweat and feel pain to become fit. Your goal is to exercise at your target heart rate for 20-30 minutes 3 to 5 times per week.

3) Always warm up to prevent muscle injury and cool down to prevent sudden drops in blood pressure & muscle soreness. A good stretching program helps alleviate muscle soreness and prevents injuries. Examples of appropriate exercises can be found on page 182.

4) Start slowly and set small goals. Pay attention to your physical condition, health, and age. If you are overweight, you're more susceptible to injuries from activities such as running. A walking program would be a better choice.

5) If you are taking medications it is important to consider the interaction between certain drugs and the body's response to exercise. Some antihypertensive medications should not be combined with exercise programs. For instance, beta-blockers decrease the body's tolerance to exercise. And, many diuretics increase potassium losses as does intense physical activity. Muscle weakness, spasms, twitching, and rapid heart beat, all symptoms of low blood levels of potassium, may result. A physician should monitor potassium levels and may prescribe potassium supplements, if necessary.

If you currently have a sedentary lifestyle, start slowly. Select any activity that you enjoy such as working in the garden, raking leaves, chopping wood, mowing the lawn, vacuuming, swimming, or even stair-climbing. Investigate local community programs, join a health club, or use a video exercise program. Work several different activities into your weekly routine. Once you have become accustomed to a more active lifestyle, you are ready to begin a more formal exercise program.

Many individuals own their own exercise equipment. A home gym can cost hundreds of dollars or as little as the cost of a jump rope. Whether you buy a few dumbbells, a jump rope, or a stationary bicycle, put your equipment in a pleasant place and use it at a certain time of day. Exercise will then become a habit at a special time of the day such as during the nightly news or a morning talk show.

As you plan an exercise program, ask yourself:

- Will the activities fit easily into my schedule? Exercising after work when you are tired might not be as successful as a walk during your lunch hour.

- Is the activity too costly? If an exercise program doesn't fit into your budget, you may find yourself not exercising at all.

- If a gym or jogging trail is needed, is it readily accessible? If walking outside, what will you do if it rains? Is a mall nearby for indoor walking?

- Do I need a friend to exercise with in order to keep up motivation? Is there an alternative if my friend can't participate?

- Is the activity enjoyable? Don't ignore having fun. Studies show most people don't stick with exercise that they don't enjoy.

AEROBIC EXERCISE

The definition of aerobic is "with oxygen." Aerobic exercise describes an extended vigorous exercise that strengthens the heart and improves the cardiovascular system. Aerobic exercises use mostly large muscles in rhythmic, continuous motions such as running, swimming, or cycling. Anaerobic means "without oxygen." An anaerobic exercise is a short, all-out exercise effort. Anaerobic exercises often isolate a single group of muscles such as in weight training and may involve explosive movements.

These types of exercises may do more harm than good and are not recommended for hypertensive people because acute and sudden increases in both systolic and diastolic blood pressure readings may occur. If you wish to use weights to increase muscle tone, light weights of five pounds or less pose no risk.

Participation in a sport does not necessarily contribute to fitness, weight loss, or improved heart and lung capacity. Sports such as golf, bowling, archery, shuffleboard, and croquet don't require a vigorous and sustained effort. They don't increase heart and lung activity enough to improve the cardiovascular system.

HOW MUCH EXERCISE
DO YOU NEED?

Aerobic exercise should be performed at between 60 to 85% of your maximal heart rate. The maximal heart rate is an estimate of the greatest number of beats per minute your heart is capable of beating. If you have led a sedentary lifestyle, aim for the lower limit as you begin a fitness program and work up to the upper limit. A good rule of thumb to remember: any exercise that works your heart at or above an intensity of 100 beats per minute can be beneficial.

**To figure your target heart rate
use the following formula:**

220 - age	=	maximum heart rate
x .60	=	target heart rate (lower limit)
x .85	=	target heart rate (upper limit)
x .75	=	target heart rate (middle level)

For example:

If you are 40 years old, your maximum heart rate is 220 - 40 or a pulse rate of 180 beats per minute. Your target heart rate would be 75% of 180 or a pulse of 135 beats per minute. Your lower limit would be 60% of 180 or a pulse of 108 beats per minute. Your upper limit would be 85% of 180 or a pulse of 153 beats per minute.

HOW TO TAKE YOUR PULSE

Your pulse rate indicates how hard your heart is working as you exercise. To take your pulse, stop exercising at the end of 20 minutes and immediately count your pulse for 10 seconds. Multiply this number by 6 to figure your pulse rate for 1  minute. Take your pulse at the wrist or neck area as illustrated. Use an index finger to feel the pulse.

To improve heart and blood vessel fitness or for weight control, experts state that exercise must be conducted at the target heart rate for at least 30 minutes five times a week. To maintain fitness, three times a week is recommended.

FITNESS WALKING

What is fitness walking? Fitness walking is walking at a brisk pace to improve your health. It is a natural, simple, easy, effective program you can do anytime. To obtain the maximum benefits from fitness walking, walk 20 to 30 minutes 5 times each week. Let your body rest two days each week but it's best not to take two days off in a row. Most importantly, before you begin a fitness walking program, obtain approval from your physician.

One Dozen Benefits of Fitness Walking:
1. Improve endurance.
2. Improve strength.
3. Improve flexibility.
4. Shape and tone the body.
5. Help control weight.
6. Improve circulation.

7. Regulate blood pressure.
8. Raise good cholesterol (HDL's).
9. Reduce stress.
10. Improve mental function.
11. Increase energy.
12. Improve mood.

What you should wear:
- Comfortable, loose-fitting clothes.
- Heavy socks to cushion the feet and to keep from getting blisters.
- Comfortable, athletic-type shoes to protect your feet and allow you to walk fast.

How to fitness walk:
To fitness walk, you should walk naturally and concentrate on:
- Standing up straight.
- Reaching forward with the legs to take nice long steps.
- Pointing the feet straight ahead and using a heel-toe action.
- Swinging the arms forward and backward to give you balance and rhythm.
- Walking at a naturally brisk pace which pushes you almost to the point of breathlessness but still allows you to talk.

When walking, practice these safety measures:
- Wear the proper shoes and socks.
- Walk in a safe area.
- Ear phones should not be used when walking out doors; they may keep you from hearing approaching vehicles or people.
- Use sidewalks when available.
- When walking on a road, stay on the left shoulder facing traffic.
- Cross the street only at crosswalks.
- If walking at night, wear light and/or reflective clothing and carry a flashlight. Walk at night with a partner.
- Warm up and cool down using the following exercises.

Warm up and cool down exercises:
- Side bends
- Hamstring stretch (back of upper leg)
- Quadriceps stretch (front of upper leg)
- Calf stretch
- Ankle rotations

Repeat each exercise 3 times. Hold the stretch for 5 seconds; do not bob to prevent muscle strain.

RESOURCES

If you would like to learn more about topics discussed in *Recipes For The Heart,* many pamphlets and books are available from public and private sources. Most pamphlets are free or can be purchased for a small fee. A partial list includes:

The American College of Sports Medicine
P.O. Box 1440
Indianapolis, IN 46206-1440

   Fitness in Healthy Adults

American Dietetic Association
216 W. Jackson Blvd., Suite 800
Chicago, IL 60606-6995

   The American Diabetes Association/The American Dietetic Association. Family Cookbook, volume 1. and Family Cookbook, volume 2.

American Heart Association
National Center
7320 Greenville Ave.
Dallas, TX 75231

   American Heart Association Cookbook, 5th Edition

   About High Blood Pressure

   Cholesterol and Your Heart

   Cooking Without Your Salt Shaker

   Facts About Potassium

   High Blood Pressure: Facts You Need To Know

   High Blood Pressure: What It Is, What It Can Do To You, What You Can Do About It

   How To Have Your Cake And Eat It Too: A Painless Guide To Low-Cholesterol Eating

   How You Can Help Your Doctor Treat Your High Blood Pressure

Now You're Cookin'

Recipes For Low-Fat, Low-Cholesterol Meals

Salt, Sodium and Blood Pressure

Strokes: A Guide For The Family

The Way To A Man's Heart

Consumer Information Center
Pueblo, Colorado 81009

Sodium Content Of Your Food (#001-000-04179-7)

High Blood Pressure Information Center
120/80 National Institutes of Health
Bethesda, Maryland 20205

High Blood Pressure and What You Can Do About It by Marvin Moser, M.D.

Blacks and High Blood Pressure (NIH #82-2024)

Microwave Diet Cookery: Low Calorie Menus for All Seasons by Marcia Cone & Thelma Snyder.
Simon & Schuster, New York. 1988.

Microwaving Light & Healthy by Barbara Methvan.
Prentice Hall Press, New York. 1989.

The Joy of Microwaving by The Microwave Cooking Institute Staff. 1988.

National Dairy Council
6300 N. River Road
Rosemont, IL 60018

The All-American Guide To Calcium-Rich Foods

President's Council of Fitness & Sports
450 Fifth St. NW, Suite 7103
Washington, D.C. 20001

How Different Sports Rate in Promoting Physical Fitness

Scriptographic Booklet
Channing L. Bete Co., Inc.
South Deerfield, Maine 01373

Living With High Blood Pressure (#1411A-12-83)

You and Your Blood Pressure (#1163K-7-84)

What You Should Know About Cholesterol (#1272C-3-84)

What You Should Know About Sodium In Your Diet
(#1294C-4-84)

Superintendent Of Documents
U.S. Government Printing Office
Washington, D.C. 20402

A Word About Low-Sodium Diets (HHS Pub. #84-2179)

High Blood Pressure Facts and Fiction

Protect Your Lifeline! Fight High Blood Pressure

Questions About Weight, Salt, And High Blood Pressure
(NIH Pub. #84-1459)

Nutrition & Your Health (Home & Garden Bulletin #232)

Sodium Content of Your Food (Home & Garden Bulletin
#233)

Sodium Count Down-reprint from summer 1986 Food News

Sodium Facts For Older Citizens (HHS Pub. #83-2169)

Sodium: Think About It (Home & Garden Bulletin #237)

Nutrients in recipes were calculated using:

USDA Agriculture Handbook #8 Series

USDA Home & Garden Bulletin #72

USDA Home & Garden Bulletin #233

Averaging nutrient contents as listed on product labels.

Nutritionist III by N-Squared Computing.

RECIPE INDEX

RECIPE INDEX
Recipes Listed By Food Group

INDEX

To order additional copies of

RECIPES FOR THE HEART

A Nutrition Guide For People With High Blood Pressure

Send order form to: Sandridge Publishing Company
                       15348 Sandridge Road
                       Bowling Green, Ohio 43402

1-10 books $13.50 each plus $2.00 shipping & handling per copy

10 or more books $11.00 each plus $1.00 shipping & handling per copy

Quantity _____ Unit Cost $ _____ Total $ _____

Shipping/Handling $_____

Ohio orders include 6% sales tax $_____

TOTAL $_____

Name _____

Address _____

City _____ State _____ Zip _____

Payment must accompany order.
Make checks payable to Nutrition Consultants.

FAVORITE RECIPES

FAVORITE RECIPES

FAVORITE RECIPES

FAVORITE RECIPES